## Advance Praise for *Lessons from the Len Master*

"Life lessons. Illustrative stories. Practical, business applications. Shared wisdom, worth sharing."

—Mark Johns, Speaker, Consultant,
Author of *Twenty Timeless Truths of Selling*
and *Successful Sales Management*

"In life, what we resist persists, so let your resistance be your compass, and experience the joy of the opportunities that open up. Ron's book shows you how resisting the temptation to do things the wrong way pays off with persistence and success."

—Andy Phillips, CEO, Cliq, Inc.

"Ron preserves the legacy of his father's wisdom in this book and I'm honored to have the opportunity to learn and benefit from it. I work hard to align myself with great leaders. I'm fortunate to follow in the footsteps of people like Ron and his father, remembering the strength that an ethical balance brings to my business."

—Zabrina Hazeltine, CEO, Hamilton
Group Meeting Planners, Inc.

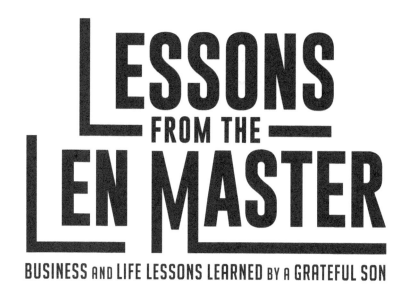

# LESSONS
## FROM THE
# LEN MASTER

BUSINESS AND LIFE LESSONS LEARNED BY A GRATEFUL SON

# RON ZAYAS

Post Hill
PRESS

A POST HILL PRESS BOOK
ISBN: 978-1-64293-429-8
ISBN (eBook): 978-1-64293-430-4

Lessons from the Len Master:
Business and Life Lessons Learned by a Grateful Son
© 2020 by Ron Zayas
All Rights Reserved

Post Hill Press
New York • Nashville
posthillpress.com

Published in the United States of America

# DEDICATION

To my wife Elizabeth, for all the love, support,
and friendship I could ever need.

To my father: Turns out, I may have been listening after all.

To Declan, Cam, and Peyton for reminding me about
the importance and joy of family wisdom.

# CONTENTS

Prologue .............................................................. ix

Twenty Years Earlier................................................ xi

Working with Don Draper's Eviler Twin ............................. xv

October 2000...................................................... xxi

My Father and Me ............................................... xxv

## Section 1: Three Lessons for Success in Business

Lesson 1: If the Powers That Be Won't Let You Play in
Their Reindeer Games, Get Your Own Set of
(Loyal) Reindeer............................................... 3

Lesson 2: Teach a Person to Learn and She Will Thank You.
Teach Her to Think and She Will Be Successful
Throughout Her Life...................................... 15

Lesson 3: People Lie. Get Over It, but Learn to Spot a Lie.
It's Easy. *Es mas facil cojer un mentiroso que un cojo*......... 27

## Section 2: Three Lessons for Negotiating Well

Lesson 1: The Aim of War Is Total Victory. A Negotiation Isn't a War.................... 39

Lesson 2: No Is Not Maybe. No Is Not a Negotiation Point. No Is a Line in the Sand, So Use It Carefully. *No es no, nunca, jamas.*.....................51

Lesson 3: You Shouldn't Punch an Angry Bear or Kill a Fly with an Elephant Gun..............................59

## Section 3: Three Lessons for Life

Lesson 1: Everything You Are Today Is Because of What You Did Ten Years Ago. So If You Want to be Successful Ten Years From Now, You'd Better Get Started.............. 71

Lesson 2: The True Measure of a Person Is What They Do When They Are Stressed................................79

Lesson 3: Never Forget Your Children Are Watching, or Your Name Is My Name...........................87

Bonus Lesson: *Hagate Hombre* (or *Mujer*)...........101

A Final Thought................................................107

Acknowledgments ...........................................109

About the Author ............................................111

# PROLOGUE

## August 15, 2000

I had been with the company five years. I was still in my twenties and advancing quickly, having negotiated my way to a director's position and then making assistant vice president. The company was profitable and a leader in its industry. My salary was decent, and with three small children and a wife finishing college, this was a comfortable situation.

And then events turned against me, so quickly and disastrously that it felt like my life became a French film. Note to non-film buffs: French movies never have a happy ending.

The Internet (it was still capitalized back then) was making companies rethink their existence, and any organization with a retail footprint wondered if they would be around in ten years. My company, old and stodgy as it was, lacked a web strategy and was too complacent to react to the changes that technology was bringing.

The former vice president of marketing was an affable guy who had a fifteen-year history with the firm. He was not digitally savvy but was smart enough to sense what was coming and jumped ship to another company. This should have been my opportunity for advancement, but a new, seasoned vice president with illustrious credentials had been chosen instead. They wanted me to stay and serve as his implementation arm and his protégé. So far, so good. Not what I wanted, but not fatal either.

Then I met my new boss, DJ. One meeting was enough to realize the guy was a desperate, sexist opportunist who had only stayed long enough at Fortune 500 organizations to avoid getting fired before moving on to dupe some other company. His one positive attribute was that he looked like a senior officer, almost straight out of *Mad Men*. Fifty years old (Jesus, that seemed ancient back then), well dressed, tan, and fit, he had tricked everyone into believing he knew what he was doing.

It started to look like I wouldn't have much of a future at this company. Fortunately, something in my past allowed me to change the narrative in my favor.

# TWENTY YEARS EARLIER

"*Check.*"

*I looked at my situation and knew it was hopeless. My father was two moves away from checkmate. I loved chess, but hated losing with every fiber in my body. Losing was bad enough; watching it happen was even worse. Half in anger and half in respect, I tipped my king over.*

*"It's not fair," I protested. "You've been playing much longer than me. I will never beat you."*

*"Probably not," he laughed. "But in life you will often come up against people who are smarter, more experienced, better looking..."*

*"I get the point," I interrupted.*

*"But that doesn't mean you can't win. Let's play again, only this time I'll tell you what I am going to do: you open yourself to a weakness when you castle [a defensive move in chess designed to protect the king]. I am going to attack you right here," he pointed, "and force a checkmate. Now that you know what I am going to do,*

*you should have the advantage. Set up the board and remember to use your knights better."*

*Unfortunately for me, the game soon ended and I was mated again. Disgusted, I pouted like the nine-year-old sore loser I was. "You changed your strategy. That's not fair."*

*"I had to, because you played like you knew my strategy."*

*"You told me your strategy," I whined.*

*"Yes. And knowing what I was going to do should have given you the game. But instead of using that knowledge to win, you squandered it. You didn't castle. That was your whole game: not castling. Once it became clear you weren't going to castle, I switched tactics and beat you."*

*"But, but…I had no choice," I stammered. "You told me you would beat me by getting me to castle. Then you changed your game. You lied."*

*"Not castling doesn't win the game. Killing my king wins the game," he scolded. "You knew what I wanted you to do. Instead of making that obvious, you should have used that knowledge to find a weakness in my defenses. Once I knew for certain that you were not going to do what I wanted, I had to change my strategy, and you lost your advantage.*

*"In real life I would not have told you my motives, but sometimes you can figure out what people are doing. The lesson is, if you know something I don't, use that to win. Don't tip me off, or I will*

change my plans. And simply not doing what I want you to do is not a strategy. Get it?"

I nodded. I wasn't happy about it, but I got it.

"And one more thing," he added, "You didn't use your knights enough. Most pieces move in a straight line. People can see straight lines easily. It's harder to see erratic movement. When you add unexpected actions, it's harder for people to guess what you will do next. That might be enough to defeat someone who is smarter, more experienced, better looking, taller…"

It was lessons like these, brutally simple, yet lovingly and patiently taught, that earned my father Len, the title of Len Master in my eyes.

# WORKING WITH
# DON DRAPER'S EVILER TWIN

My first planning meeting as an assistant vice president was held at a nice beach hotel. I still distrusted my new boss, DJ, but I was excited about being included in the planning process. The company was actively looking to protect itself from the changes tearing at the old tapestry of the print and franchise industries, but no one had a clue what to do about it. Like the twenty-something that I was, I felt I did. They needed direction, I had it, and this was my chance to prove I was a valuable asset.

If I could show that I had a plan, and that DJ was clueless, perhaps I could still get senior management to change course. DJ was making his mark by critiquing everything and everyone in the marketing department without really having a constructive strategy. Morale was down, and caution was the rule. People were more concerned about protecting their jobs than innovating and risk taking; that's bad for a company at any phase, and fatal for companies at transition points. If your people are too afraid to try something, you are doomed. This was my chance to influence the plan.

Then fate intervened.

Upon our arrival at the hotel, another junior officer and I were directed to the wrong meeting room—the one where the senior staff had already planned next year's strategy. Everything was laid out on easels and notepads. Ironically, neither the technology of planning nor the strategies they came up with had changed since the 1950s. Once I speed-read the bullet points and charts, the overall narrative became clear: stay the course and hope we survive another year.

My coworker grasped what had happened: we were set up. Today's meeting would be a Potemkin village of thinking exercises and strategy sessions, and would end exactly as was outlined on these walls. They didn't want our opinions; they wanted us to believe our opinions mattered. "Well, at least they aren't planning on firing us," he joked.

I was a bit more disappointed. In fact, I was angry. My first temptation was to walk in, throw their notes on the table and expose the charade. I would outline their faults, their bad planning, and then end with a short and concise "Fuck you. You deserve each other. Like the Titanic, keep playing the same music until the ship sinks." Satisfying? Yes. Constructive? Not so much.

But then I remembered I had three children. We had outgrown our small rental house. My wife was not earning money yet and was about to graduate with $60k in student loans. Whether this company survived or not, I could still get paid and chances were that, with DJ in charge of marketing, I would be indispensable. Job security is a great thing when you have a family to feed. All I had to do was shut up. I looked at my coworker as we walked to the room where we were supposed to have gone, and understood exactly what he meant. Shut up and collect your check. But I knew I couldn't pull that off. Plan A was looking better by the minute.

That's when I heard the inner voice that I knew belonged to my father: "You know something they don't know you know. If this was a chess game…"

It was definitely his voice, that melodic, Cuban-accented voice that I had heard all my life. In my mind I even heard "some*sing*" instead of "some*thing*," just like my father would say. Although I hesitated, his advice was irrefutable.

So I decided to go in and be my father, despite the strong pull of my ego and the competing interest in just doing nothing.

I opted for the Columbo approach—not tipping my hand by exposing what I knew, but asking relentless questions to ramp up their discomfort. As the meeting droned on and the executives became bored, ready to run toward their already-developed strategy and call it a day, I continued my inquisition.

*"I don't understand, how will doing this stop competition from the Internet?"*

"We can't control what our competitors do," DJ condescendingly explained, "but we can focus on the fundamentals that have made us successful. Serve our customers. Conserve our cash. Protect our bottom line."

*"But what if doing things online is easier or cheaper for our customers? If we lose customers, don't we lose our cash and our bottom line?"*

"The future is a train coming at us, Ron. The brands that will survive are the ones with a 'wow,' and that make customers trust them like their moms, which is 'wow' upside down."

As God is my witness, I am not making this up. That was the actual conversation. "Wow upside down is mom." Brilliant!

My questions were targeted and direct. I played the part of someone who was ignorant and wanted to learn, but to my boss I was merciless. His empty platitudes, vague strategies, and promises of magic solutions would one day propel him to the White House (Okay, I made that part up), but for the life of me, I couldn't understand why no one else was seeing this.

*"I don't understand what you want me to do exactly, can you explain that again?"*

"Yes, be innovative, but remember our roots. Don't ignore the competition, but don't let them define who we are."

*"Hmm, sorry, I am being thick, but when we get back to the office on Monday, exactly what should I do differently?"*

"Nothing. Well, everything. Well, just follow the plan."

*"Now we are getting somewhere. So what is the plan?"*

"Stay the course."

*"Stay the course?"*

"Stay the course. We have a plan—just follow it, damn it!"

*"Gotcha."* At that moment, I looked around the room and realized I wasn't the only one who knew my boss had no clue. I went from feeling like I was the protagonist in a depressing French film to being held over the bow of the Titanic and feeling like I could fly. Exactly like that. Well, *somesing* like that.

# OCTOBER 2000

Eventually, in private and away from DJ, the president and the CEO each talked to me about my plan. Convinced that I had one, they asked me to prepare a strategy which would be reflected in our new website. I consented but attached two conditions: I would work alone, and I would present my results to the whole group without having to go to my boss first. They agreed.

I also had a deadline: I had accepted an offer with another company (yes, an internet company), and had only thirty days before I was scheduled to start.

**Len's Rule:**

**When you have your opponents by the balls, squeeze just enough to make them know it, but not enough to make them your (castrated) enemies for life.**

I spent the next thirty days writing out all facets of an online strategy. I mapped out the key points, budget and implementation, and a skeleton of a proposed new website, including server-based functionality that every retail center could customize locally. On my last day at the company, I presented my findings to the senior management.

The questions in the room came fast and furious as they tried to take in the changes we needed to implement. "How will we get the franchisees on board?" "Is this a marketing or a technology strategy?" "How can we train our employees to do this?" I answered as completely as I could—I wanted them to succeed—but time was running out and eventually I would have to leave. Unless they made the right decision, in which case I could stay and put this plan into action.

For the marketing-centric among us, my strategy was simple: our upstart competitors had innovation, a clean slate, and technology. We had experience, profits, and a physical footprint. If we gave up all of that to only compete online, we would be playing to their advantage. If we combined our physical locations with a strong, modern website and made technology easier for our franchisees, our clients could decide how best to interact with us. We already knew what our competitors' strategy was going to be, so we needed to use that to our advantage.

The three-hour meeting stretched an hour longer and no one wanted to leave. But I had a deadline (another great piece of advice from my father: have your exit planned). "I am sorry, gentlemen," I said, bringing the meeting to a close. "I promised my wife I would eat lunch with her on my last day. My job is done. My notes are here. You guys are bright. You'll figure it out."

Before I left the room, a senior manager I respected stopped me and said, "You are about to get asked to lunch by the president. Please accept his invitation." I called my wife and asked her permission to cancel lunch (family first was one of *my* rules), and accepted. By the end of that lunch I was the newest and youngest VP of marketing in the company's history. I had a hefty raise, a nice bonus for a down payment, and a mandate to build a new staff—*my staff*—for the work ahead. In short, my father's advice got me everything I wanted.

Would I have left? Yes. Did I want to leave? No. In the end, it was a perfect negotiation: both parties got what they wanted and no one was a loser—except for my former boss who was sent packing that same afternoon. I could see my father smiling from two thousand miles away.

## It Helps to Have Good Parents

Parents give children a lot of advice: look both ways before you cross the street, wear clean underwear, and never marry a woman who thinks Tom Cruise is an actor. (That last one wasn't from a parent, though sage advice nonetheless.) But how many parents teach their children to sell, negotiate, get a better job, or run a business?

Mine did.

My father was an involved parent and taught me the life lessons that are the core to how to act, how to read people, and how to get what I want in my career, fairly and justly. Those lessons started with my earliest memories and have continued over the decades of my life. I have written them down, condensed them, and added examples of how you can apply them in your career. Whether you are an employee wanting to move up, a salesperson looking to close more sales, or a manager or owner looking to better run your company, I think you will find these lessons useful.

So, if your father (or mother) never taught you how to spot a poser from across the room, how to be confident, or how to lead others to help accomplish exceptional goals, this is the book for you.

The lessons are divided into three sections: rules for getting ahead at work, effective negotiating, and increasing your ability to achieve your goals, and a bonus section with one of the most profound things my father ever taught me. Does it help to have a Hispanic background and know a little Spanish? That's how the lessons were imparted to me, but they can help anyone looking to succeed in business while also becoming a better person.

# MY FATHER AND ME

If you are going to get advice from someone, it's important to know something about the source.

*Len*

My father's accomplishments start with being a good father: learned in many subjects, a talented writer, and an exceptional salesperson. He succeeded at what he tried for the most part, and was never afraid to try something new. He's intelligent (and still sharp at eighty-something), plays music, reads voraciously, has an innate understanding of technology, plays a mean game of chess, and can spin a yarn. And spin. And spin. I sometimes wonder how he smoked for fifty years, has COPD, and still talks for hours without seemingly taking a breath.

My father was a soldier who fought in the Cuban revolution, a rebel who wanted the US out of Cuba and a dictatorship overthrown. After the revolution, he grew unhappy with the course things had taken and resigned from the rebel army (something thought to be impossible). He started a new career in movies, producing newsreels and eventually feature films, a lifelong passion he never forgot. He emigrated from Cuba to the US in the mid-1960s and eventually settled in California with three kids, a wife, and the challenge of learning a new language.

He made his living in sales, something that came naturally to him, and eventually migrated to the hardware side of the new computer industry that was taking shape in the early 1970s—working with computers instead of selling something. After years in his adopted career, he became ill to the point of being told to put his affairs in order; he was dying from a disfiguring disease that doctors couldn't treat or even explain. He checked himself out of the hospital, and when he returned a few months later the condition was gone, and he was determined to change his life. He retired before the age of fifty and still managed to earn a living doing software development and sales, writing blogs, and developing websites.

Most importantly, he always set an example that in life you need to go your own way. It sounds trite, but strength is less about being aggressive or violent, and more about understanding who you are and not being intimidated by others. Or, at least, never *acting* intimidated.

*Me*

I have never been motivated by money, but I love to sell. As a kid I sold lemonade because it was fun to provide something that people wanted. Rather than open a lemonade stand in front of my house, I took a thermos and a supply of Dixie cups (my mom worked for Dixie at the time and I don't think we ever owned real plates and glasses), went on my bike to schools and soccer fields, and sold cold refreshments onsite for a huge profit. That's how I learned that if you combine a need with convenience, you have a business model.

At nine, I sold Avon for my mother door-to-door (I still smell a little like lavender). I also sold greeting cards to purchase a chemistry set I wanted (you haven't lived until you try selling Christmas cards to strangers in July). I excelled at school fundraisers, and even helped my friends sell their items when they weren't doing it correctly.

By high school, I had convinced our local team sports administrator to let me staff events with reliable workers I provided and made a couple of bucks commission on each hour they worked. I started college at sixteen, and I was running the school newspaper—and its $300k annual budget—before I was eighteen. I was a student government senator, then senate president. I started my first business a year out of college when I was barely twenty-one.

Since then I have alternated between working as a marketing vice president and CMO, and starting, running, and selling my own businesses. In the last fifteen years, I have started multiple successful companies, and currently own and run a profitable marketing and technology firm. I have written several books, and have been invited to speak at business events across the US and in other countries.

And I couldn't have done half of that without my father's lessons.

As my father says, *"guerra avisado no mata soldados,"* which basically means, just shut up and get to the point already.

# SECTION ONE:

# THREE LESSONS FOR SUCCESS IN BUSINESS

Getting ahead in work is important to lots of people, because work is where we spend most of our waking hours, and because earning a living is critical to the other parts of our lives. But I have found that true success—being happy with the decisions you have made and where they have gotten you—is interwoven with all aspects of life. Personally, I don't think you can feel good about your life if you made a lot of money, but were a horrible spouse, parent, friend, or human being. That's the important thing about the lessons I learned from hearing and watching my father; they taught me to be a self-made, better person.

YOU CAN'T GET INTO SOME CLUBS. FORM YOUR OWN CLUB. FIND OTHERS WHO ARE BEING LEFT OUT, FORM ALLIANCES, AND PROMOTE EACH OTHER. HELP EACH OTHER. GET THE RECOGNITION YOU WANT, AND LESSEN THE POWER OF THE PEOPLE IN THE CLUB.

# IF THE POWERS THAT BE WON'T LET YOU PLAY IN THEIR REINDEER GAMES, GET YOUR OWN SET OF (LOYAL) REINDEER.

## Another Lemonade to Drown My Sorrows, Please

For more than ten years, Lisa had been a great worker at the company. She moved up from an assistant's position to a manager, working long hours and letting her organizational and team building skills overcome every obstacle. She took on new responsibilities, completed projects on time, and rarely took individual credit. But eventually she found her growth path blocked, her pay stagnant, and officer-level promotions going to more aggressive fellow employees.

Those employees weren't more talented or industrious, but they were closer with senior management. They socialized with them, and, whether it was talking about politics, going hunting for small animals, or slugging back hard liquor after work, they just went with the flow. But not everyone is able—or willing—to sacrifice family time to get ahead, or has the stomach to shoot a pheasant with a shotgun at point blank range.

At the local Chili's, the haunt of our mid-level managers, Lisa went into the details of her latest annual review as the salads hit the table. "I went in and told Stan how much I added to the company. I listed results. I brought up all of the projects I was responsible for and how they reached or exceeded our KPIs."

A tall, attractive woman with a warm wit and well-cultured manner, Lisa seemed ten years older as her shoulders wilted from her own words. "He wouldn't budge from his 'five percent is a great raise' line. He was done with the review and was anxious to move on."

"Have you thought about taking a negotiation class?" Martina asked, trying to be positive. She understood Lisa's frustration since she was on a similar career path. After eight years at the company, she was a trusted employee, but her salary and title never matched the wonderful *atta-girl*s she received at her reviews. "We women could be better off if we were more aggressive and asked for money better."

Christina, the third member of our party, jumped in with an opposing view. "I have an MBA, and I know how to negotiate. I have saved the company hundreds of thousands of dollars in vendor costs. But if you are not in the good ol' boys club, you don't get noticed. It's like the only projects that matter are theirs."

The table grew somber and the other conversations from the restaurant started to overtake our gloom.

Finally, Lisa looked at me, the only male at the table. "You're quiet," she asked me solemnly. "You think this is a woman problem?"

My mind skipped back to the day I was a cub reporter in college so many years ago.

## Picture This: Las Vegas, in the Summer

*The blistering Las Vegas sun bleached the color from everything it touched. The calendar said March, but in Vegas the season was simply "prelude to hell." In the desert heat, under the searing metal of a car, my father and I were both trying to make an old British roadster run.*

*My father took the lead, as he always did, wearing overalls that kept him clean but were so hot and clingy they could have made a Sumo wrestler thin after a few hours in the 110-degree heat. He was relatively young then—in his forties—with his baseball cap to protect his bushy hair, and a potbelly that was the end result of five decades of Cuban cooking. Moving around constantly, he would call for tools, while explaining what he was doing. Most days I watched carefully, wanting to learn everything I could and make this my project, but today I was lost in thought and feeling sorry for myself.*

*"¿Que pasa?" he asked, seeing me distracted.*

*"It's the newspaper at school. The reporters who are friends with the editor get the best assignments. They help each other. I get assigned articles on feral cats. It's not fair. I'm a better writer."*

*"Sure you are. And over time, when those guys leave, you can get your chance. Now pay attention. Today, you can worry about fixing that," he said, pointing towards the car.*

*Ignoring him, I persisted. "I don't want to wait. I want to be editor-in-chief before I'm eighteen and I can't do that if I can't get exposure."*

*"Pobrecito," he smiled. While saying "poor little guy" sounded like he was sympathizing, it actually meant "stop acting like a child and get to work."*

*Seeing my lack of concentration, my dad banished me to the driver's seat, where my job was to try the starter out as he made corrections to the wiring. The car was on ramps, and he was underneath, so any mistake could prove fatal. My father's engineer's eye for sweating the small details, along with his innate need for self-preservation, made him yell out the series of repetitive steps every time:*

*"Put your foot on the brake. Take the car out of gear. Make sure it's out of gear. Turn the key."*

*A simple click told us we still didn't have the adjustments right and would have to try again.*

*"Okay," he shouted out, his words slurred by the omnipresent Camel filter cigarette he kept between his lips. "Turn the key off. Put the car back in gear and take your foot off the brake." I complied and waited for the cycle to repeat again after some minor adjustments.*

*Twenty minutes and ten rounds later, the master mechanic shouted out again. "Put your foot on the brake. Take the car out of gear. Make sure it's out of gear. Turn the key."*

*I heard the words, but my brain didn't follow the simple directions. Instead, I robotically turned the key. For those of you that have grown up with automatic transmissions (or electric cars), you have to understand that if you have a stick shift car in gear and you turn the key, the starter moves the car. Of course, on this try—the only one I forgot to take the car out of gear on—my father had found the right combination of adjustment. The starter engaged; the car lunged forward, went off the ramps, and fell on my father.*

*The consequences could have been life threatening. Thankfully, the ramps held, stopping the car slightly above my dad's body as the front tires slid over the ramp. My father slithered his rotund figure out from under the car faster than I had ever seen him move, his face white with fear. Once the adrenaline ebbed, anger took over and my father began spewing profanity at my utter carelessness.*

*And it would have been intimidating, were it not for the comical look of the broken cigarette dangling from his mouth as he spoke.*

*I laughed. He uncharacteristically controlled his violent temper and retired to the apartment to cool down.*

*Eventually, as he always did, he returned with a new set of procedures and steps intended to ensure his safety. But before we started again, he had me explain my situation at the newspaper. If he was going to survive, he needed me focused.*

*After listening patiently, he sighed. "You can't get into some clubs. Friendships and work relationships are forged over years. Sometimes they don't let you play because you don't look like them, or because you aren't like them. Sometimes it is just because they trust the people they know. The trick isn't to become like them. Be you. But that doesn't mean you have to do it alone. Form your own club. Find others who are being left out, form alliances, and promote each other. Help each other. Get the recognition you want, and lessen the power of the people in the club."*

*Not what I wanted to hear, but it made sense. I smiled, only to be brought back to earth a second later.*

*"Now pay attention, you idiot. If you screw this up again I will set this piece of crap on fire and go back inside where it's cool. I have a car and I don't need to get killed fixing a bad one. And you owe me a new carton of cigarettes."*

## Meanwhile, Back at Chili's

Lisa repeated her question: "Ron, you think this is a woman problem?"

"No," I answered, coming back from my daydream. "This isn't a woman issue; it is an outsider issue, although it is probably harder on women. The officers and their friends are always together, and a lot of the real decisions are made long before we even hear about them. Plus, they trust and like one another, so of course they stand up for each other. We don't get shout-outs, so it seems we are not important. That's the problem."

"Yeah," Martina sighed. "Maybe I should take up hunting."

"Or maybe we need to create our own team," Lisa said.

Lisa picked up on what I was saying and ran with it. By the next day, she came back to the four of us and had a list of rules for being in *our* club:

1. *Help your team members out.* If you can help them be successful on a project, do it.
2. *Call out your team members whenever possible.* If you have the mic or spotlight, use it to acknowledge a contribution from someone else on the team.
3. *Always put your teammates' projects ahead in priority, if you can.*

4. *Never speak ill of others on the team.* If you have a disagreement, solve it quietly. Acknowledge in public, and admonish in private.

5. *If you move up, remember your team members.*

In reality, the top management had been doing this for years, but for them it evolved organically. They did it because they were friends or were related. We had to try a little harder, but it had the same effect. Suddenly our names came up more often and we created our own buzz. It helped that our team members were hard-working and talented, and that ability started to get noticed. Over time, it meant more high-visibility projects, more promotions, and more money for all of us.

Not a bad return on an $8.25 pack of Camel filters.

## Putting It into Practice

We are social animals. We hunt more successfully in packs, and we have evolved to work better as a team. If you doubt that, try staring down a woolly mammoth on your own, you skinny little ape. But in a group of humans, we hunted these giants to extinction.

Wait, that's not good.

The point is: why forego the advantages of being in a supportive group, just because someone else decides you are not pledge material? While your first instinct may be to go it alone, the rewards of cooperation are too numerous to ignore. And if you work in a place too small to create another team, look for support in associations or other organizations. If you have people helping you find a better job or environment, that works as well as advancing at your current job.

What builds a team? A shared vision? Attitudes and affinities? DNA? Probably all of these things. As such, it is easy to understand why some teams get cliquish. I worked at a company where most of the officers had the same last name (I was also convinced there was some inbreeding going on, but could never quite prove that despite the unusually high incidence of hemophilia). It was easy for them to be a team; they loved and trusted each other. Letting others in was more difficult. They ran the company, they made the promotions, and they decided who got paid more. But even in a situation like this, a few of us outsiders were able to work together. Over time, we became a team of winners. We weren't *their* team, but we were hard to ignore because of our successes. We got noticed. And when some of us left for greener pastures, our team members naturally sought to follow. The ones that stayed behind got treated better because they were too valuable to lose.

You can live your life trying to figure out a way to marry into the royal family, or you can run for parliament and succeed on merit, not bloodlines. There is nothing wrong with being born into the right family at the right time. But if you're not, it's not the end of the world.

One final note: once your team becomes a functioning, cohesive whole, and/or when you become the team captain, don't forget how it felt to be outside the "in" crowd.

IF YOU STRUGGLE WITH THE
CONFIDENCE TO LEARN NEW THINGS,
ASK YOURSELF HOW WHAT
YOU ARE LEARNING IS LIKE
SOMETHING YOU ALREADY KNOW

# TEACH A PERSON TO LEARN AND SHE WILL THANK YOU. TEACH HER TO THINK AND SHE WILL BE SUCCESSFUL THROUGHOUT HER LIFE.

## Let's Just Take Her Out to the Desert and Leave Her There

Eliana's frustration was evident by the scowl on her face. As COO of our nonprofit division, she understood how to make things work. She oversaw accounting, HR, and operations, and often saved me from my own bad financial decisions ("You know what would be great, Eliana? If we rented the space next door so we could expand and build a game room for the employees!").

She tended to be no-nonsense and expected the same from her team. Today she was doing Naomi's review and just couldn't find the right words.

"Every time I write her a review," she explained, "it comes out worse than expected. I want to say, 'you are good at what you do, but you are challenged when you have to try new things.' Instead it comes off as 'Perhaps you should work at McDonald's.'"

I motioned for her to hand me the review. I quickly read through it and handed it back. "Actually," I said, "it comes off more as 'you'd be lucky if they hired you at McDonald's.' Is that what you really think?"

She shook her head. "When she is good, she is high-value. She is conscientious, dedicated, and can be trusted. But sometimes she hits these walls and becomes, well…" her voice trailed off.

"You can say it," I said. "It is just the two of us."

"Stupid," she mumbled.

Personally, I was thinking she was going to say "less than efficient."

"Do you think she is stupid?" I asked. You could see that Eliana immediately regretted her choice of words.

"No," she sighed. "She just gets stuck, and is difficult and defensive because she is scared at being in over her head. Every time I give her a new assignment that she thinks is way out of her experience, she gets agitated. But I need her to learn new things. She has grown a lot, moving from customer service to accounting, but if she wants to be a manager, she needs to move forward on her own. She needs to think somehow, and I don't know how to teach someone to think."

"Exactly," I said, while getting up and closing my door. "Which reminds me of a story about my dad."

Eliana's eyes glanced at the closed door and knew she was doomed. Sulking into her chair, she feigned enthusiasm for yet another long Ron story. But seeing that she was trapped—and knowing I would be reviewing her next month—she faked a smile.

*It's good to be king*, I thought to myself and sat down.

## Dinner at the Zayas Household, Circa the Ancient '70s

*Dinner at my house was never about eating. In fact, the food was never really that good. Cuban cuisine has its high watermarks—especially around holidays—but day in and day out, you basically ate rice, beans, and meat. Vegetables? Forget it. I am amazed I never had scurvy. Dinner was about the family getting together and my parents using our native language and conversation to impart culture. It lasted two hours, if you were lucky—if my father was on fire it could go three hours or more—and we covered topics from politics to religion, from music to art. I grew up thinking these were marathon torture sessions, but later realized they were how my father and mother subtly molded our minds and taught us to think.*

*As long as I can remember, I wanted to learn to fly. Not with angel wings and pixie dust (that was just a phase), but in a small plane. My father had been a pilot, self-taught, and judging from some of his stories, not a particularly good one (in case the term "self-taught pilot" was not enough of a clue).*

*One day I mentioned how I thought learning to fly would be difficult. My father stared at me for a moment while the table was cleared, his espresso steaming from the comically small cup in which it was traditionally served. He started the inquisition. "Why do you think it would be hard?"*

*"I don't know," I groaned, using my best little kid sarcasm to tick off reasons. "Because it takes a lot of training. Because if you screw up you kill people. Because it is fighting gravity and taking a really heavy object and making it soar." I was incredulous that a man who had both flown on his own and was deathly afraid of commercial jetliners would ask such a stupid question.*

*"I see," he said pulling a careful sip of the liquid tar from the coffee cup. He let the hot liquid roll over his tongue, before using the baby spoon to add a miniscule amount of sugar and slowly stir it in. "What if I told you that you already knew the basics of flight? What if I told you that you do what a pilot does every day?"*

*I laughed. My father had a gift for theatrics and hyperbole—I am almost certain he once told us he had discovered the microprocessor and invented a way for all computers on the planet to com-*

municate with each other. But I was having none of it. "You would be wrong. I don't fly a plane. I don't even fly toy planes."

"Hmm. But you ride a bike, right?"

"Yes," I agreed cautiously. "But a bike is not a plane. It is not even close."

"I see, Mr. Wright, you know everything about flying," he said, using his best adult sarcasm voice.

"No I don't," I protested, "That's my point. I don't know anything about flying."

"That's obvious," he continued. "But you do know how to ride a bike, right?"

"Of course," I said proudly. "In fact, I doubt anyone rides a bike better than I do." I said this partly because I lived on my bike, and because, growing up watching Evel Knievel, I could do wheelies, jump trash cans, and go off-roading. And I had the scars and broken rims to prove it.

"Planes gain lift from speed," my father interrupted. "The air passes over the wings quicker on top than on the bottom, which creates a vacuum and lifts the plane. Bikes use speed as a gyroscopic force to keep the bike up and straight. You do know how to keep the bike upright, no?"

I nodded.

"You steer with the handlebars; a pilot uses a yoke."

At this point he was on autopilot and no more input was needed from me.

*"Like a pilot, you use speed and yaw to keep the bike on course. You balance yourself, changing the weight and position of your body depending on whether you are going uphill or down, or what pilots call pitch. And when you decide that you want to stop, you come to a controlled standstill so that you stop upright and do not fall down like you did when you were first learning. Pilots call a landing a controlled crash. You have to slow down enough to land, but not so slow that you stall and hit the ground. Any of this sound familiar?"*

*My cue: stop daydreaming and nod.*

*Very happy with himself, he went for the close. "Any idea of what the Wright Brothers did for a living before they invented the airplane? Or do you not learn anything in that fancy school you go to?"*

*"They made bicycles," I mumbled unenthusiastically.*

*"You think that was a coincidence? You already know a lot about flying. And what you don't know is like what you didn't know when you started riding a bike. You will learn. Look around at the people who fly planes. Are they any smarter than you? Any better? If they can do it, you can. Now get me some more coffee."*

## It's Not Siesta Time at Zayas Industries

Seeing Eliana about to nod off, I raised my voice slightly to signal my story was done.

She snapped back to attention. "So riding a bike is like flying a plane. I get it. Thank you. May I go now?"

"No, the lesson is: one thing is generally like another. When we find connections between the things we know and the things we don't know, we have more confidence in expanding our experience. It is a way of thinking that humans have used for a million years of evolution. But you have to learn how to think like that. Teach Naomi to think, and you will find her to be an extremely loyal and dedicated manager."

"Teach her to think," she said matter-of-factly. "So rather than just give her new assignments, explain how what I want her to do is like something she has done before?"

"Well," I said, tilting my head to let her know she almost had it.

"Let her make the connection. Don't tell her, lead her there."

"Exactly!" I smiled.

"That makes sense. By the way, you could have just said that and saved me a twenty-minute story," she laughed.

## I Recite These Words to Myself When Confronted with a New Situation

Some of the greatest discoveries in our past were based on someone applying a concept they knew in a different way. A battery and a watch spring are a lot alike: fundamentally, they store energy. A plane and a ship share much more in common than terminology. And when someone eventually builds the warp engine, chances are they will discover the principles based on something they already knew. That is the core of thinking, of genius, of humanity.

If you struggle with the confidence to learn new things, ask yourself how what you are learning is like something you already know. Once you find a corollary, learning the task will be easier. Ask yourself:

1. *Has anyone ever done this before?* My father taught me to drive stick by putting me in a car and saying "Have you seen the people who drive manual transmission cars? If they can do it, you can." While extreme, it stuck with me. If someone else figured this out, it can be done. If them, why not me? And if someone has done it successfully before, there must be something I can read or watch to get me started.

2. *What is this like?* Does anything about this task seem familiar? I hate accounting, but as a small business owner, I have to understand the principles of debits, credits, revenue, expenditures, cashflow, and profit. Anyone who has ever been broke understands those concepts. We do them in life every day to make ends meet. My first sales job started out disastrously until I started thinking about

sales being just like dating. Unfortunately, looking at dating being just like sales doesn't work so well.

3. *Do I have time to get help, or do I need to do something now?* If you have time to find a mentor, or read up on the problem, there is no shame in that. The Middle Ages lasted so long because literacy had failed and people had to learn the same lessons again and again. Today, we have no excuse for not learning from the successes and failures of others. But if you don't have time, get your mind in the right frame and think your way out of the situation. As one of my best green, three-foot tall mentors once told me, "Do or do not. *There is no try!*"

Part of this lesson is learning to think. The second part is teaching others to think. Whether it's your child, employee, or manager, you need to give people the tools they need to solve problems for themselves.

I use these steps to help others think:

1. *Use the Socratic method.* That's just a fancy way of saying "Teach them by asking questions." Ask the same questions you would ask yourself. Get them to make the connections.

2. *Point them in the right direction, but don't shove them.* Ask this way: "Well, you did accounting at your last job,

and here we need you to help organize production. Is there any part of your prior position that required organization?" Not this way: "You stupid little monkey, you did inventory when you worked in the warehouse and now I'm asking you to inventory software we own on our computers. It's the same fricking thing, you moron." Trust me: number one works out much better.

3. *Suggest resources.* An employee of mine had gotten into the habit of asking his supervisor for answers, and when that supervisor went on vacation he started pestering me instead. I gave him a set of things to try before he could come into my office asking for help: 1) Have you ever done anything like this before? 2) Did you Google it to see if someone else has done this before? 3) If I wasn't here and your life depended on making the right choice, what would you try?

4. *Make them present you with options, not problems.* This forces people to think. I simply tell my employees that I will help them choose between options, but won't allow them to present me problems. This worked really well with the employee in the previous example. It was difficult for him at first, but once I trained him on the previous steps, he got better at solving things on his own.

Thinking is what makes us human. Thinking allows us to imagine things we have never seen before or may never have experienced. How much time have you devoted to learning to think?

WE KNOW WHEN PEOPLE
ARE LYING, WE JUST NEED SOME
HELP SOMETIMES FOR OUR BRAINS
TO CATCH UP TO OUR GUTS

LESSON THREE:

# PEOPLE LIE. GET OVER IT, BUT LEARN TO SPOT A LIE. IT'S EASY. *ES MAS FACIL COJER UN MENTIROSO QUE UN COJO.*

## He Should Be Writing Emails for Spammers

*Larry Luis.* I remember the name of this former employee so well because his lies caused us to almost lose one of our biggest clients, one that accounted for $1 million a year in sales.

Luke, Larry's supervisor, came in one day with doubts about his employee.

"There is something not right with that guy, Ron, but I am not certain what it is," Luke said, while eyeing the candy dish on my desk.

"How is his work?" I asked.

"It's okay. But sometimes he skips a step, and if I bring it up, he mentions that he did do it and just forgot to update the code. Or that it isn't necessary because of this or that. I am not sure I feel he is being truthful. If I can't trust him, it's an issue because I can't check 10,000 lines of code, but if I am wrong, I am giving him a bad rep without proof." Luke leaned forward to grab a handful of M&Ms.

I forcibly slapped his hand away. "Stay focused, man. Have you ever caught him in a lie?"

Luke thought about it while rubbing his now-stinging hand. "Not really. Well, not anything *major*."

"Define *major*."

"I asked him if he had completed a project and he said yes and that he would show it to me tomorrow. Needing it now, I just went up and checked the code, hoping to save some time. It wasn't there."

"And when you asked him about it?" I said, while helping myself to some red M&Ms. Remembering I was vegan, I put them back.

Luke looked up, angry that I was toying with his love of chocolate. "He said he had meant to say he was 'going to finish it tomorrow' and that I misunderstood. But I am sure I heard him correctly."

"We have an issue," I said. "He has a liar's vocabulary."

"A what?" Luke asked.

"People who lie have certain habits, and vague vocabularies are one. Have some M&Ms and let me tell you a story." Luke hated stories, but loved M&Ms, and was content to put up with one for access to the other.

## Sometime in the 1990s

*Four years out of college, I had just sold my first company and was looking for a new job after blowing through the proceeds of the sale. Wanting to move back to Southern California, I had a couple of offers. One started at a lower salary, but the opportunities seemed more abundant, at least to hear the CEO tell it. The second job paid better—and had better benefits, but was more mundane. I was young and single and I was more interested in doing something interesting than making a lot of money. And the first job had this incredibly lovely receptionist.*

*I was certain I was going to go with the first job, but I took the time to speak with my father about my interview with the CEO before I made a decision. He offered some surprising insight.*

*"You can't trust that guy. He is a liar," my father said matter-of-factly. I discounted the advice, and was even a bit annoyed at it—the presumption that my father could tell someone was lying by proxy. I sat with the guy and did not pick up any lies, so how could he?*

"You don't even know him," I countered. "How would you know he's lying?"

"Because you know he's lying. You just told me four lies he told you. You are just not paying attention, or at least not paying attention to the right thing."

These were the traits that really upset me about my father: he had an opinion for everything, and was so certain about his conclusions. "Really. I don't remember saying he was lying about anything."

"Four things," he said smiling. "First than nothing"—that's not a typo, he actually says that randomly for some reason—"you said he told you that he was very successful and that the company was growing and profitable. But then you mentioned that when he put his feet up on the desk towards the end of the interview, he had a hole in his shoe, right?"

"Yes, and that is odd, but not a lie. Maybe he is too busy to get new shoes," I said lamely. Truth is that had bothered me, too, I just hadn't put it together until now.

"You ever have a hole in your shoe? Drives you crazy, so it is not like you could ignore it. If he wanted to bring you on board, and had other shoes, he would have changed, or not put his shoe up. But he's too lazy to do one or the other, or doesn't have other shoes. Liars are lazy and people with struggling companies might be tight for cash."

Lucky-ass example, I thought to myself.

"*Second, you said he took you on a tour and that there were empty desks. When you looked at them, he said, 'Oh yeah, we have people out today attending training.' He also mentioned later how busy they were. You wouldn't have a lot of people out on training at the same time when you are busy. I mean you could, but it doesn't add up.*"

I nodded. It had bothered me enough to mention it to my dad, and he had caught that.

"*Third, he uses a lot of 'we are gonna' sentences. We are gonna do that, gonna do this. Liars live in the future, not the past, because they seldom have a list of accomplishments. He didn't take a lot of time to show you things they had done, right? Just things they were going to do?*"

I nodded again. I was feeling really badly about where this was going.

"*Lastly, he told you lots of times how successful the company was. You mentioned it three times.*"

"He mentioned it more than that," I added.

"*Figures. Liars will always tell you the opposite of what they want you to think. They know what they are lying about and are sensitive about it. So, they repeat that and make it seem like it is no big deal or so obvious that you shouldn't even look into it, because they don't want you to look into it.* Es mas facil cojer un mentiroso…*"

*By the way, that Spanish phrase in the title of this chapter means: it is easier to catch a liar than it is to catch a man with a limp. I realize how politically incorrect that saying is, and I apologize if it offends anyone. If I were to modernize it I would say it is easier to catch a liar than a cold at a preschool, but I am not in charge of Cuban sayings.*

*I got the point. I wanted to believe him, and to think that a successful company really wanted me that badly, even though I didn't have a lot of experience at this point. Another lesson about liars: they say what you want to hear.*

*All the things my father worried about, turned out to be prescient, I know this because I took the job anyway. Not only was the business in economic distress, the owner eventually had tax and lawsuit issues that crippled the company. So why on earth did I take a job when my father's advice was so against it? Did I mention the beautiful receptionist? Two years later, we were married, and to this day, marrying her is the best decision I ever made. Father doesn't always know best.*

## No, Luke, He Is My Father

I finished and looked at Luke, ready for him to thank me for sharing my father's wisdom.

Luke stared at me intently—as intently as he could with a mouth full of melted chocolate. While I was lost in the details of my story, he had managed to eat the entire bowl of M&Ms. Jerk.

"I kinda think he's lying," he mumbled. "So what do I do?"

"Check up on him and give him some sunlight. What project is he working on?"

Luke looked down at his notes, timid about his answer. "He is working on securing the website for our largest client. We need to make certain that it can withstand intrusions, so I gave him our procedures on hardening the forms. He has been working on it for two weeks."

"That scares me," I said.

"Me, too. I'm going to review his code tonight and meet with him in the morning. If I am wrong, no harm. But if I'm correct…" he trailed off.

"I don't think you are wrong," I added. "We know when people are lying, we just need some help sometimes for our brains to catch up to our guts."

"I know, but I see the pattern," Luke smiled. "I wonder if it's too late for me to change the way I voted on my absentee ballot."

It didn't take long to find out the extent of Larry's deception. Luke reviewed the work and found almost nothing completed. He asked Larry about in the morning, and Larry demurred saying he had not uploaded the code yet. Luke went to Larry's computer, and, searching it with him, found nothing. Larry was sure the files had been accidently deleted. *Right.*

By the time we got it all sorted out, Larry was fired and our client's job was delayed but at least it was done correctly. It could have been a lot worse.

### Remember these rules on spotting liars:

1. *Liars are lazy.* It is one of the main reasons they lie. They cut corners. If you suspect someone of lying, check the work. You will start to find things that are not done and procedures that are not followed. It's a pattern. They take the easy way out.

2. *Liars don't like questions.* Keep asking questions and eventually you will break a liar, because they pride themselves on thinking on their feet. It is hard to remember things you just made up.

3. *People who lie a lot think they are good at it.* They get cocky, and they get even lazier. When you think you are good at something, you seldom invest a lot more time getting better at it.

4. *Liars lie about stupid things.* They lie about unimportant things. They mostly lie because they are lazy or afraid. But once they discover that lies help them get out of things, they become addicted. I mentioned to a coworker once

how interesting his shirt was. He told me an exotic story about how he had it custom made. I laughed. I spotted the shirt because I had the same exact shirt from Lands' End. Nice shirt, but not exactly the "made by the thread of a silkworm hand-fed by a Thai peasant" kind of shirt he described, either.

Is it important to know someone is lying? Of course. Business—and life—is about trusting others. Lies get in the way of our trust. It doesn't mean that anyone who lies is a liar, but liars lie to specifically harm us to their benefit. You can't be successful in life if you can't spot and defang liars.

# SECTION TWO:

# THREE LESSONS
# FOR NEGOTIATING WELL

Negotiations aren't about getting something at someone's expense. Any fool can do that. Negotiations are about understanding what the other party needs, knowing what you want versus what is fair, and coming to a lasting, mutually beneficial agreement. You ever do a deal and then realize later you were taken? Ever do business with that person again? Exactly.

These next three lessons will ensure that you cut deals you won't regret, while keeping other parties engaged and working towards your success.

"I AM GLAD YOU LEARNED THE MOST IMPORTANT PART OF NEGOTIATING—UNDERSTANDING THE OTHER PERSON'S POINT OF VIEW AND GETTING TO SOMETHING THAT WORKS FOR BOTH OF YOU."

LESSON ONE:

# THE AIM OF WAR IS TOTAL VICTORY. A NEGOTIATION ISN'T A WAR.

## Sometimes You Just Want to Win

Artemus understood he had been screwed. He had been promised a partnership and he worked hard for the company. He was making a good living and getting a fair share of the profits he helped generate, but he wasn't a *partner*. He didn't own anything. If his "partner," Austin—the real owner of the company—decided tomorrow that Artie was out, his profit sharing would end. If Austin sold the company, Artie would be left begging for a share of the proceeds, since he had nothing in writing to say he was entitled to anything.

I tried hard to bring this point home to Artie on multiple occasions, but he trusted Austin—until the day Artie insisted he needed to be a partner with equal equity, *now*. "It's only fair," Artie told him, "I account for sixty percent of the profit and this company has grown over the last few years because of me."

Austin showed his true colors. "You're not an owner, Artie. I am, and I don't feel like I should share the company I started. You get profit share. It's just as good."

Artie called me that day looking for advice on how to get even with his business partner. "I have already decided I am leaving, but I am in a good position to hurt him in the negotiations. If I take all of my clients—and they will go with me—he will go out of business. Not having anything in writing works both ways. I have no limitations on what I can do. So, I want a big payout and commission. Help me get there."

It's tough when someone asks for advice and you know the best way to help is not to tell them what they want to hear. Attacking his partner was not the smart thing to do. Even if he received a good severance package, Austin didn't have the money to buy him out and would have to pay over time or fight Artie in court. And Artie didn't have the stomach or money for a protracted court case, and couldn't trust that if he bested Austin completely, that his former partner would faithfully execute any agreement anyway. Artie needed to get some value for what he had developed, and then go on with life. Breaking badly with Austin was not going to help. As usual, it reminded me of this one time when my father first taught me how to negotiate.

## The Fun Starts When You Get the Top Off

*There was never any doubt about what my first car would be, and when I spotted a 1970 baby blue MG Midget convertible for $1,000, I was already picturing myself in the driver's seat cruising beaches in Southern California with the top down. Problem is, I had to get the guy to come down 50 percent on the price. Enter Len, the negotiation sensei…*

*True to his nature, my father was not going to help me without some form of quid pro quo. There was a lesson to be learned here, and he wanted me to pay attention. So, before we headed out, he went over the game plan.*

*"What do you want out of this?"*

*"An MG Midget for $500. Or less."*

*"What does he want?" he asked.*

*"To sell the car for $1,000."*

*"So how do you get him to come down in price?"*

*"We haggle. We beat him down. We make him think the car is shit and he is lucky we would even spit on this car, much less give him $1,000 for it."*

*"No. Listen, Ron. He wants to sell. This isn't the kind of car you buy because you need it. You buy it because you love it. You put*

your heart into it and want to keep it forever. But if you run out of money, or you have to pay rent, or your kid needs to go to the doctor, you sell it. You have to and you want to get what you can, but deep down inside, you would feel good if it went to someone who will love it, too."

"Got it. He needs the money. Prey on that. Find the wound, stick your finger in it, and twist it until he gives us the car."

"No! What is wrong with you? We ask him what he has done to the car. That will tell us what he hasn't done to it, and where we will need to spend money. This has to be fair to you, too, and the truth is you only have $500. If we need to do $300 worth of repairs, we have to get this car for $200 so you have $300 left to fix it. Understand?"

"Yes," I nodded, although this didn't sound like a negotiation, it sounded like a math lesson.

"I will talk more than I usually do so you can learn from this. You just hand him the money when I tell you. You are scaring me with all of this crazy 'finding the wound' talk. Oh, and one more thing: you have to be willing to walk away from this. If you can't do that, then don't go."

"But I want this car!" I protested.

"No, you want a car you can enjoy and drive. There is a difference. Don't forget that."

Armed with the cash from my first student Pell grant that should have gone toward books, we showed up at a 1950s-style block home in a less-than-nice neighborhood in Vegas. As two small kids played in the yard, the owner of my car came out to greet us. I loved the car. I had named it before the guy even started the engine.

It purred roughly (okay, it gasped and wheezed like my grandfather on a treadmill), but it started. My father egged him on about all the after-market touches on the car, and the man gladly explained the money and hours he had spent repairing it. But when my father asked to drive it, the man became less confident.

"The master cylinder is shot, but that's an easy repair," he explained. "You can rebuild it for $25."

"Well, not being able to drive it brings the value down a bit. I can't really tell how it is going to drive, or what shape the shocks or the alignment are in," my father countered.

"Yeah, but it's still a steal at $1,000."

My father didn't hesitate to counter his faulty logic. "But the truth is, if it was an easy $25 fix, you would have done that, knowing you'd get more money for a car that runs, right?"

The man sheepishly nodded his head.

"Still, it's a fine car," my father talked out loud while he carefully continued his inspection. He pointed out every flaw, but conceded the ones that were minor and easily fixed, while making note of the cost of the major ones. The owner objected to some, but eventually followed my dad's lead. First rule of any negotiation: my father had come prepared. He read up on the MG and studied its faults (basically anything from the tires up).

*After a long conversation, and well over an hour outside with the car, my father was ready for the close.*

*"Harrison—may I call you that?" The man nodded, although I wasn't certain that was even his name. "It's a nice car. But it doesn't drive and has some faults. My son is no mechanic, but this is a simple car to learn on. Still, to get it running, it will take money. I can give you $250 for the car, right now. We will have it towed, but we will have to use your phone. We didn't know that it didn't run. You have put a lot into this car. We will give you a fair price, and get out of here. A month from now, we will come back so you can see what we have done to it and you can even take a ride in it. Do we have a deal?"*

*Harrison shook his head. "No, sir. The car has its faults, but it's worth $1,000. Maybe $750, but at $250 you are trying to rob me."*

*"Sir," my father said slowly, "no one is arguing what the car is worth. You put in a lot of time and money. But the car still needs work. I am telling you what we can honestly afford and still get the car on the road. You can tell me that you don't want to sell it for $250, and that's okay. But I don't want to be selling this car three months from now because my son ran out of money. I want this car to run, and I bet you want to cut your losses and get some money out of this deal."*

*The man struggled. He looked inside to his home, hearing his wife's voice, and his trepidation grew. "I have other offers that are more than that. How about $500?"*

*My father walked up quietly to him. "Take a moment and discuss with your wife. If she doesn't want to take the money and wants you to keep waiting to sell it, we will leave and find another car. I get it. You can take one of those offers. But if not, we can each get what we want today."*

*The man nodded and walked inside.*

*"There is no way he is going for $250," I whispered.*

*"He has no choice," my father said, without a hint of happiness, "There are no other offers. We have been here for an hour on a Saturday and the phone has not rung and no one has come by. We are his only offer, and he knows that a car that doesn't run isn't worth anything. He is out of money and time to fix it. She will see that faster than he will. He will tell her if he can just fix the brakes, he can sell it for more. But she has heard that before. She just wants it gone."*

*On cue, the man emerged, his wife walking him to the door. Defeated, he quietly asked for $300 and my father agreed. They shook hands and I went inside to make the call for the tow truck, while the man gave my father the papers. Inside his wife looked at me and said "I hate to do that to him. He loves that car. But we have rent and kids. Three hundred will at least help with some of the rent. I appreciate you guys giving us the extra $50."*

*I don't know what happened next, but I walked outside and told my father in Spanish to give him the $500. My dad, confused, took me aside and asked why.*

*"Five hundred dollars is fair. They need the money. I can always work a job for the additional repairs. Do you think $500 is fair?"*

*My dad nodded. "I am glad you learned the most important part of negotiating—understanding the other person's point of view and getting to something that works for both of you."*

## Jesus, Am I Paying for This Call?

Back on the phone, Artie was exasperated. "I don't care about buying a crappy car. Will you help me get this guy or not?"

"I'll help you succeed. So just think about this for a moment: you are starting your own business in the same industry as Austin. What are you going to need to get going?"

"Clients," he interrupted.

"You need the good clients, the ones that are most deeply tied to you. And you need references. That includes explaining what you have done for the last few years of your life. Anyone can look you up on LinkedIn or Facebook and see that you worked for Austin's company. What makes you think they won't check with him?"

Artie became uncharacteristically silent.

"Exactly. So decide what is fair for you and for him. Cherry-pick your clients, and remember you need to talk with them, too. They may decide to stay put and you can't change that. Give

Austin your demands. Explain why it's fair and see it from his point of view, too. If he decides to not do the right thing, then I promise I will help you find his wounds and I will personally stick my thumb in them until he screams. Deal?"

"Wow," Artie mumbled, "your dad is right, you have issues."

## Take These Lessons into Negotiations

You have two choices when you go into a negotiation: adversarial or mutually agreeable. In business, I think most should be the latter. Sure, when you buy a car from a dealer, the silly antics, stunts, and semantics they use make the situation seem like a street brawl. But in the end, you want to buy a car and they want to sell one. You don't want to pay more than the next guy, and they don't want to go out of business. Start from that, and you can get to "yes" a lot faster.

More importantly, when you don't make negotiations a life or death struggle, you might form relationships that last far beyond the negotiation. You get more ROI from a win-win relationship.

1. *Do your homework.* If it is important enough to negotiate, it is important enough to know what you can about the job, the offer, or the person. Even an honest person doesn't have to tell you the potential pitfalls. That's your job. Ask someone who has done this before, or some-

one who has been in a similar situation about what they learned *after* the deal was closed. For example, ask anyone who has bought a boat, and they can tell you dozens of things that will save you a bundle before you buy yours.

2. *Think about what you would do in their shoes.* Would you sell at their price? What would worry you about the negotiation? Get beyond focusing on what you want, and think about why they are selling their business, offering you the job, or doing a request for proposal. If you think like them, you will be better at finding flaws or pitfalls.

3. *Don't ever make a major decision without sleeping on it.* If the offer won't be there in the morning, it is not a good offer. If anyone tells you that to make you act now, it is because if you had more time, you wouldn't buy it. No good offer ever started with "order within the next five minutes..."

4. *Talk to someone you trust and try selling the offer from the other side.* In other words, role play (not that kind of role play...*focus!*). They will tend to be dispassionate and find better negotiation points. If your friend consistently walks away from the deal, maybe you should, too.

5. *Think about the big picture.* What happens after the negotiation is done? A friend bought a company from a man who had owned it for twenty-five years. He beat the man down and got a fantastic price. But it was complicated

to run. After such a harsh negotiation, the former owner was in no mood to help the new owner out. When you think about what may happen down the road, you may want to do the right thing, and not just what you think is best for you.

6. *Take the right deal, not the best of the worst.* Anyone who has ever hired someone learns this the hard way. When you hire the right employee, good things happen. When you hire the best of the worst, it turns sour quickly. The same goes with negotiations. A deal that seems better than your options is likely to fall apart anyway. Sometimes the best deal is no deal.

If a negotiation becomes a battle, chances are everyone loses. I prefer to view it as the start of a relationship. Unless you are buying a used car, in which case, find the wound, put your finger in, and push until you get the price you want. (Why is it that no one likes that line but me?)

NO MEANS NO. IT IS GOOD ADVICE IN LIFE, AND IT IS ALWAYS GOOD ADVICE IN BUSINESS. IF YOU LET "NO" MEAN "MAYBE," YOU LOSE THE ABILITY TO LET PEOPLE KNOW WHEN THEY HAVE CROSSED THE LINE.

LESSON TWO:

# NO IS NOT MAYBE. NO IS NOT A NEGOTIATION POINT. NO IS A LINE IN THE SAND, SO USE IT CAREFULLY. *NO ES NO, NUNCA, JAMAS.*

One of the most important lessons I learned from my father wasn't actually a concrete memory, but more of an ongoing observation. My father can be loud, boisterous, and have the temper of a constipated bull at a Mao flag festival, but when he said no, it was almost Zen-like. If you were to picture an animal saying no, my father's delivery was like that of a shark—coldly precise. His "no"s were plain and Spartan (with a capital S), but something about the way he said it made you understand that there was no moving him beyond it.

I came to understand that "no" was an atomic bomb of words: you try to never use it because it is so overwhelming in effect. But if you bring it out, you can't—or shouldn't—walk it back. In a way, "no" is like your reputation. If people believe you when you say it, they won't tend to question your authority.

Although we never specifically spoke about it, I learned from my father that your "no" had to be unequivocal in business and in life.

## A Million Reasons Not to Say No

One of the first companies I started was a graphics consulting company. Fresh out of college and rather unsophisticated, I stumbled onto a profitable business by accident. Even my hourly fee was set on a fluke: I asked my girlfriend what number she would like me to charge and she suggested an impossibly high (for us) number. I decided to charge that, and people paid it.

The work was hard but fulfilling, and with no employees and a few good clients, I was making a lot of money. Then one client in particular started to want more, and soon I had a few employees and overhead, payroll, and accounting tasks. We grew with other clients, but this one in particular outdistanced the rest. By the end of the year, they accounted for 40 percent of our revenues and 60 percent of our profits. They liked us and we were a great fit for them.

Then one day, they asked us to expand our services in a way that made me uncomfortable. I had started the business and grown it based on what I knew. Tommy, the COO of our client's organization, wanted us to go in a whole new direction. It would mean hiring experts and bringing people on board in a field I knew nothing about. He offered us a contract, but I just couldn't get comfortable about it. At what should have been a celebratory meeting to sign a new agreement, I let Tommy know we couldn't help.

He was as direct as he was polite. "If we can't have you do it, we have to find another company. If that company does what you do for us now, we will also go with them on those services. You sure about this?"

I nodded. "I just don't think we would be good at it. I understand the risk, but I have to say no."

He noticed the hesitation in my voice and preyed upon it. For whatever reason, he wanted us to take the offer. He led off with solid reasons why it was in our best interests to proceed. I told him I had considered these reasons but wasn't comfortable. Then his tone changed to a hard sell, his insisting that my "no" was a repudiation of the entire relationship—and his decision to hire us in the first place.

A big, intimidating guy who looked like he could have worked for the Gotti crew, his professional, educated façade began to slip. Something about this was ticking him off. As he became more insistent, I knew I had to say no, and I could hear my father saying "say it like you mean it."

So, when he stopped talking, I calmly said, "My answer is still no. Nothing you say is going to change that." With that, I got up and started to walk out, when Tommy started in again.

"I am not done talking," he said.

Without turning around, I opened the door. "But I am."

By the next day, the damage was done. We got a thirty-day notice ending our agreement. I was looking at having to let half my workforce go in thirty days, and these were not just my employees, they were my friends.

Stopping by my parents' house on the way home that night, I explained the situation to my father, hinting that maybe I should reconsider. My father, usually the voice of reason and reconsideration, was adamant. "The time to reconsider was before you said your 'no' was final. Once you said that, the damage to your reputation is more than the damage to your company."

"Tell that to the people I have to fire," I mumbled.

"I understand," he said. "Next time you will be more careful before you shut the door. But once you do it, you have to stand by it. Plus, I don't think you were wrong. Something about this is worrying you. You are probably right."

It was not the answer I wanted to hear, but I took his advice. We lost the account, lost a quarter of our staff (I managed to save a couple of jobs by hustling new accounts), and it took us a year to get back to where we were.

I saw Tommy at an event two years later. He was gracious and welcoming, and asked about business. I didn't play off the fact that losing them was a blow, but we had survived.

He laughed. "It was the right decision. You weren't ready for it, and neither was the company that I hired to do it. I was worried about this, and I wanted you to take the job because I trusted you. I knew you would tell me if something was going badly. The other company—not so much. But you stuck to your guns, and I respect that."

I smiled. "So can we get the account back?"

"No," he said, and turned back to his tablemates.

## A Few More "No" Tips

No means no. It is good advice in life, and it is always good advice in business. If you let "no" mean "maybe," you lose the ability to let people know when they have crossed the line. Don't use it indiscriminately or you will paint yourself into a corner. Negotiations that get to "no" have generally failed. But if those around you understand how seriously you take "no," they will respect you when you use it and work to avoid getting there in the first place.

A few more "no" tips:

1. *Think about it before you say it.* Do you mean no or maybe? If you mean maybe—which is fine—say so. Lead with "Yes, if..."

2. *When you say no, don't yell it.* Say it softly. One of the things I learned from a mentor in college was that if you want to get someone's attention in a crowded room, whisper. People will strain to hear you.

3. *What if you really meant no, but someone's argument is convincing enough to make you change your mind?* It happens. Acknowledge it and explain why you are moving from "no" to "yes." Far from making you seem weak, I think it increases the respect others have for you when you can admit you are wrong.

4. *In my experience, while I may delegate "yes" to other employees in their dealings with clients and vendors, I guard "no" very closely.* If that is what a client needs to be told, I'm usually the one who does it. I can position it better and be certain that it is expressed in the way it was intended. Over the years I have found that when I have to get involved in that manner, my clients and vendors step back and ask about ways to get to yes, rather than entrenching their positions.

# IN A NEGOTIATION, WINNING IS GETTING TO YES. THE *RIGHT* YES.

LESSON THREE:

# YOU SHOULDN'T PUNCH AN ANGRY BEAR OR KILL A FLY WITH AN ELEPHANT GUN.

If you play chess, you know the elegant simplicity of the game. You start out with the same pieces in the same placement. Both players see each other's moves, and each piece can only move in a limited way. The only arguable advantage is who gets the first move, and you take turns doing that. So you would think the game would end in a draw 99 percent of the time. But it doesn't (well, not at the level most people play). So how do you win at chess? By anticipating the next move.

The best players don't just guess individual moves—they also guess outcomes. When you run enough "What if?" scenarios, you find that if you make the right moves, the steps may change, but the ultimate outcome turns out the same. My father was a master chess player.

## Ocean's Four

A company I started after college involved selling high-end computer design and consulting. We had a novel way to get from idea to finished printed piece for 50 percent of the cost of traditional methods. And we were good at training people to do it. We weren't selling technology, software, or hardware. We were showing people how to do things better. Employees got retrained instead of replaced and learned new skills; employers saved a bundle.

*What an easy sell*, I thought. Except we were kids barely out of our teens, and we had no customers, no references, and no successes. But I was lucky enough to have attended college in Las Vegas. The president of the university, an incredibly supportive and genuine person, knew a donor who was married to a casino magnate. The president introduced us to her, and she got us in to meet with him. Never say luck is not a superpower, because some of the most definitive moments in my business career involved lucky breaks like this.

Our messaging for the meeting was direct: we will train your people for free. Who can miss when you are selling something free?

Once I had my pitch in place, I decided to run it by my father (actually, I was hungry and wanted to eat at my parents' house, and this was as good an excuse as any).

## Don't Ask if You Don't Like the Answer

*My father destroyed our sales pitch in minutes: "Put yourself in his place. What if he doesn't believe you? What if he doesn't think you're old enough, smart enough, or professional enough to pull it off? Do you think he will risk his reputation on something just because it's free? What do you think when you hear free?"*

*Sure, Facebook, Google, Instagram, et al., have made billions from free (or at least making you think your information is free), but he was right. "Free" can sometimes mean worthless or cheap. Considering his position and stature, even if we could save his casino 50 percent on design and printing costs, that was hardly worth his time. Perhaps he'd listen if he was a print manager or a purchasing agent, but this guy was the CEO.*

*We were missing step one in any negotiation: put yourself in your opponent's shoes. After a lot of soul searching we focused on giving him a strategic advantage: our system got him to market faster with promotions and marketing materials, and allowed him to version his documents to better target his audience. Armed with a new pitch, I tried it out on my father. He was intrigued.*

"Interesting," he said. "That is a good idea. But I will pass. I'm too busy right now."

I was crushed. I was even more upset because I did not have a plan to overcome the most basic objection ever. I left dejected, but vowed to come back.

Two or three tries later we had overcome the "no time" objection but got stopped at "What if my employees won't change?" And then at "You have never done this before." As my frustration level grew, my father waited patiently for my eventual epiphany.

"This is stupid, and you're stupid, and you have no idea what he is going to say. You are just being a prick!" I screamed. And there it was, one man's moment of clarity is another man's temper tantrum.

My father was frustrated with how badly I was missing the big picture. "You are focused on overcoming objections. That works with bad sales pitches. You are talking to someone who knows you have more to gain from this than he does. You are not going to sell him into this."

I stared blankly.

"Just knowing what he might say next isn't enough. You need a strategy that gets him to yes. Winning tiny battles does not win the war if he says 'no' and means it."

Crickets. Silence. Not getting it.

"Okay, analogy time: in chess, if you put your queen in a threatened position and with no protection, what will your opponent do?"

"*Take my queen,*" I offered confidently.

"*Exactly. And does that win you the game? Does knowing what he will do next, does that get you closer to winning?*"

"*Not without a queen.*"

"*Right,*" he said, looking around for a cancer stick. "*It is easy to guess what an opponent will do in a certain situation. But you want to get him to a specific outcome, even if he doesn't do what you expect. Get it?*"

"*Definitely understand that in chess. Not sure how it applies here,*" I said, brushing the toxic smoke from my face.

"*Breathe, Len,*" he reminded himself, after calling me a feces-throwing primate. "*Focus on what you want him to do. You want him to give you a try. To let you implement this. The objections don't matter, the strategy does. You can concede some of them. You can win some of them. But ultimately, you want to get him to say yes. And to do that, you have to have a strategy that speaks to him.*"

That sunk in. "*So, I have to play to beat him. And, in this case, beating him is getting him to say yes. And I have to understand I can't force him into it, I can't trick him into it, and I sure as hell am not going to shame him into it.*"

"*Correctamundo,*" he said. For some reason, Fonzie had made quite an impression on my father a couple of decades after jumping the shark.

"*I have to get him to convince himself.*"

*"¡Si, animal! You got it."*

*"How does a high-powered CEO convince himself in a negotiation? He talks himself into it!"*

*"Exactly,"* he coughed (we were on cigarette number two by this time). *"Even if he comes up with an objection that you can't answer, let him answer it. Tell him you hadn't thought of that. Let him solve the problem for you. If he gets excited about the puzzle and solves it himself, you win. All you have to do is make sure that the potential in what you are offering is clear. If he gets that, let him convince himself."*

*"Okay, that makes sense. But no one ever does that in chess."*

*"Not everything is a chess game, Ron. And, by the way, I wouldn't lead with free. If he likes the idea, he will pay for it."*

## Less Whine, More Cheese

It worked. We had the meeting. We presented the idea. He got excited and then started to punch holes in our plan. When we got stuck, we said we were stuck, and gave him the ability to solve his own dilemma. Being a smart, experienced person, he usually did. And when he couldn't, he just said "we'll figure that out later." We walked out of there with his blessing to try it on his staff. And we did. The only part of my father's advice I didn't take (completely) was the free part. I still said I would do it for free, sort of.

"How much will this cost?" the CEO asked.

"A lot," I answered. "But not money. If we do this and it works, you tell three other CEOs about how you did it. Not your competitors, just people you know we can help. I can't afford to buy your recommendation, but I am willing to earn it." Cheesy, but it worked, because cheesy or not, it was sincere. We did our part, and his was one of the first casinos to modernize its design department. He kept his word, and our business was launched. And to top it off, he even paid us for our time. A *fair* price. We both got what we wanted, so it was a perfect negotiation.

## So How Do You Get to Know Your Opponent?

People, especially salespeople and good negotiators, tend to have tricks to getting people to "yes." Some wear power colors, or try to show dominance by moving in close or raising their chair higher than yours. But a negotiation is not a trick. Winning a concession is useless if you don't get the ultimate objective. It is not about taking a queen—it's about winning. In a negotiation, winning is getting to yes. The *right* yes.

1. *Be prepared and do your homework.* If you don't know anything about the person you are negotiating with, you are not ready to negotiate.
2. *Put yourself in their shoes.* What do they want?

3. *Forget about what you have to gain.* Think about what success means to them.

4. *Know what you want, and at what point you are willing to walk.*

Then use this information to devise a personalized strategy:

1. *Words matter.* Choose words that are loaded in a good way, based upon your opponent's likely background, and avoid those with negative connotations. Imagine saying "broad" when meeting with Oprah Winfrey, or referring to someone in your organization as a "stupid millennial" when meeting with Mark Zuckerberg. But using terms like "self-made," "decisive," and "risk-taking" can be very positive in both these examples.

2. *Decide what "yes" is to that person and work backwards.* Role play. If yes is getting the other person to sell you her business at a certain price, think about how the person would do that and feel good about it. Then move backwards in the conversation to understand what to say to get her there.

3. *Don't worry about little concessions if they move you closer to yes.* Example: when negotiating with a prospective employee, some people value a title over a few more bucks. Some want an office, an assistant, or some perk

that makes them feel valued or esteemed in their life partner's eyes. Find those points and trade them for moving in the right direction. The more personalized the concession, the more value it has.

4. *Ask questions.* You would be surprised how much you find out by asking questions during a negotiation. We once helped a client negotiate the purchase of a business. I asked the seller what he pictured retirement to be like. The seller went into an emotional story about how his wife was ill, and he needed to care for her for however long she lived. We used that information to structure payments that allowed him to earn an income and cover extra expenses. It also allowed our client to better manage cashflow after the acquisition. The more you know, the better off you are. Just don't expect that every question will be answered—or answered truthfully.

5. *Don't stop focusing on the end result.* Remember that it is not necessarily getting the lowest price or getting the best of the other party. It is about getting an outcome that can survive the long run.

# SECTION THREE:
# THREE LESSONS FOR LIFE

Why include life lessons in a business book? I think being good at most things in business involves knowing who you are, and being the person you (and those around you) can be proud of. If you won't do the right things in your personal life, it is unlikely you'll do them in business.

This section is about what my father taught me about life, and how to apply it to business. If only he had saved me from getting that mullet in sixth grade...

IF YOU CAN PICTURE
YOURSELF AS A CEO, OR A
C-LEVEL EXECUTIVE, OR JUST A
BETTER SALESPERSON OR MANAGER,
START PLANNING TODAY TO BE
WHERE YOU WANT TO BE.

LESSON ONE:

# EVERYTHING YOU ARE TODAY IS BECAUSE OF WHAT YOU DID TEN YEARS AGO. SO IF YOU WANT TO BE SUCCESSFUL TEN YEARS FROM NOW, YOU'D BETTER GET STARTED.

66 I want to be a comedian," my friend explained to me one evening. I smiled. I had always wanted to be a comedian and wrote comedy in college for the newspaper and radio station. I have also written stand-up bits for friends. My first book was a humor book, and God knows I have made a lot of women laugh in my life for all the wrong reasons. Maybe that last part can be edited out before publication.

The thing about my friend is that he chooses careers like other people choose socks. There was a cartoon I remember as a kid about a turtle who always wanted to be something, and he would ask his friend Mr. Wizard to make him a construction worker, or a doctor—whatever—and it would happen. And the turtle realized that jobs are hard.

Steven was that turtle.

"I can go on the road. There are so many clubs out there and I'm not really doing anything right now anyway. All I need is a good routine to get going."

"And balls of steel," I added. "It's hard being a stand-up comic. I went to open mic once, with killer material, and I almost peed myself."

Steven stared down at me as if I was still wearing those same pants. "I can do it. Will you help me?"

"Sure," I said. "But first a short story."

## "10" Wasn't Even a Good Movie

*One of my father's favorite lectures involved tracing your life back to explain how the stupid thing you just did (leaving the garage door open overnight, losing your lunch pail, committing a class 2 felony, etc.) really started years ago. He would painstakingly retrace your steps (in real time, it seemed) with long lectures.*

*As a ten-year-old, you find it hard to believe that the reason you were getting grounded for the summer was really based on decisions you made in vitro, but as I got older, I started to see the logic.*

*At twenty-six, I sold my first company and was ready to start again. I wanted to leave Las Vegas and go anywhere else. I was single, my parents had moved to Texas, and I really had nothing to keep me anywhere. What a great time to just make a stupid, fun decision! Assuming you don't have a killjoy for a dad.*

*"So, what are you planning to do?" my father asked as we watched the streetlights flicker on outside my sister's home.*

*"Nothing. Travel, maybe. Jump in my MG and just drive for a year."*

*"How old are you, thirty?" he asked. My father has always had an inability to remember the ages of his children.*

*"Twenty-six this year. I have plenty of time to find life, I guess."*

*"What do you want to be doing when you are thirty-six?"*

*"Thirty-six? No idea. Maybe married. One kid. Be a writer."*

*"You may find those things cancel out. But, if you want to be that when you are thirty-six, don't you think you should start now?"*

*"Now? No way, that is a long way away."*

*"How long do you think it takes to be a writer?" he asked.*

*"I don't know," I responded. "A year?"*

*"How about to become a great writer? Does that take a year?"*

*"I am not even sure, but taking a year off seems like a good way to find myself and gain experiences that would be interesting*

to write about. It's not like I will be writing boring business books; I want to write the great novel of my time."

"True," he said in that tone that meant 'I sound like I am agreeing with you, but I'm not.' "But that is different. If you want to be a writer ten years from now, and you are taking this trip now, think how it can get you closer to being a writer. That is very different from just jumping in the car. How you look at the trip, where you go, and whether or not you take notes is different depending on whether it is for fun, or to become something."

"Can't you just let me have this one thing?" I asked, dejected and overwhelmed with how hard things seemed.

"No."

Over time, I realized he was right. Some people spend their entire lives perfecting their professions. I also realized the number ten comes up a lot. Stand-up comics, I am told, take ten years to hone their onstage personality. Doctors study for an average of ten years to even begin to enter their specialties. I think my father was on to something. I could go on that trip for fun (which is okay, too), but if I had a dream to be a writer in ten years, why not start now? It changed the way I envisioned the trip and experienced it. Some day, I might actually even write about it.

## I Still Don't Get It

Steven was having none of it. "Ten years to become a comic? That's a long time."

"Yeah," I said. "If it were easy, everyone would do it. Most people are funny in one aspect or another."

"Even programmers?" he asked.

"*Most* people are funny in one aspect or another," I corrected myself. "If you want to do this, you have to start acting like a comic now. Learn what they do, how they started out and start being like that. In a year, you can hit the road, and maybe a few years after that you can really be a comic. You're only twenty-three, you have time."

"Hmm. That sounds like a lot of work."

Cue the turtle.

## You Usually Hit What You Aim At

In business, it starts with having a plan on where you want to be ten years out, or even three years out. If you can picture yourself as a CEO, or a C-level executive, or just a better salesperson or manager, start planning today to be where you want to be. And then think like that person.

RON ZAYAS

The old adage is that writers write. A friend and business associate of mine has written dozens of books. He writes from home and he writes well. In fact, I sometimes wish I had done much of what he has done. But all of my planning and steps were to become a CEO, and that is what I am. I thought like one, acted like one, and throughout my professional career tried to look at experiences as either moving me closer or further away from that objective. As such, I never became the writer I wanted to be, or that my friend is. But since I want to be one when I retire, I am acting like one now.

We are not talking about wishing. When you wish, you use phrases like "It would be so cool to...", but when you plan, have a different lexicon. People working towards a goal want to learn more about how people who achieve their success got there. They take on responsibilities, find mentors, and practice whenever they can. They may fantasize about the perks, but they never ignore the work.

Do you want to be successful at something? Start planning now. Want to know how you got to where you are now (good or bad)? Look back at the decisions you made over the last ten years and you should see a straight line to your present. If ten years is too hard, try one year, or three.

I recently trained an eager new salesperson with no sales experience. The product he was selling for us had a long sales cycle. While he wanted to picture himself being successful—earning commissions, having flexible hours, and working with people to solve their problems—I had him instead define success and work backwards.

Five new clients a month would help him earn the lifestyle he wanted. Reasonable. So how many qualified prospects must he reach every month to get five new clients? Twenty-five? Fifty? How many cold prospects lead to twenty-five qualified ones?

He discovered how many phone calls he had to do each day—*that day*—to start his journey and achieve his goal. We also celebrated the steps that would eventually get him closer to his goal. If he needed to talk to twenty-five cold prospects today, when he reached that number we celebrated. Getting a qualified prospect was another celebration. Each tiny success got him one step closer to his ultimate success.

It's no different in life. With the future being murky, sometimes it's hard to commit today to something so far into the future. But time is going to pass anyway. Eventually, you will be ten years into the future. You will be older and you will be in the year and time that you imagined so long ago. The only question is, where exactly will you be?

PEOPLE CAN MAKE
BAD DECISIONS IF THEY FEEL
THEY ARE DESPERATE AND HAVE NO
WAY OUT. BUT THANKS TO MY FATHER,
WHEN THINGS HAVE GONE BAD, I HAVE
BEEN ABLE TO STOP A MOMENT AND
ASK, "IS THIS WHO I REALLY AM?"

LESSON TWO:

# THE TRUE MEASURE OF A PERSON IS WHAT THEY DO WHEN THEY ARE STRESSED.

Stress kills. It makes people fearful and cautious. It can also tell you the true measure of a person. Psychologists and marriage therapists will tell you that if you want to see if a relationship can go the distance, don't look at couples when they are happy; focus on how they fight. Couples that can argue, get mad, and still respect each other will generally last. Couples whose fights devolve into name-calling and personal attacks won't go the distance.

How your client, boss, or coworker acts when things are going smoothly doesn't tell you anything about them. The same is true for you. When you have a lot on the line, when you are risking your business, job, or that big commission, how are you then?

## Diapers Aren't Just for Babies

After the birth of our third child, things started to get complicated and stressful. My wife was in college and not working, and I had left my job because the company was not secure and I was bored. Of course, I had another job lined up before I left, as a general manager at a well-established diaper company. (Cloth diapers. And no, this was not 1949.) The president, a crusty old man who smelled of embalming fluid and mummy bandages, wanted to retire, and I was to take over as president in a couple of years. I was his selection, and I was already picturing how to get out of the diaper business and contort this company into something a little less scatological.

Then things went to hell. I fired a vendor who was under-performing, and it turned out she was having an affair with the aforementioned dusty pharaoh. I refused to back down, but he was much more content with his forty-something girlfriend than his twenty-something new hire. I was fired on Halloween.

With no savings, the country in the middle of a recession, and three small children, I was worried. Everyone depended on me, and while I knew my wife would quit school and do whatever we needed to survive, I didn't want her to do that. I always glibly said that any problem you can solve with money wasn't a problem, but now I needed money, rent, food, healthcare, and gas, and it started seeming like a big problem. I know people go through this every day. I know many people in the US are financially insecure. But this was new to me. Not because I had never been poor, but because I'd never had so many people depending on me.

With no credit, wealthy friends, or parents with nice investments, I was on my own. My choices were to sell a kidney or find a new job. And I could only sell a kidney once.

Not finding a job in my field, I grew desperate. I applied at a Blockbuster video store and got turned down, because I wasn't qualified enough (seriously, he said I had no video experience). *Sigh.* I took a part time job as a database administrator in the weirdest company ever. Ostensibly a youth placement service for study-abroad kids, the president would seal himself in a bullet-proof office each day and only come out to berate the four women who worked for him. Sexist and aloof, he would go into a rant until I would say "enough," and then he would go back in his panic room. I would tell my coworkers they didn't have to take this, but they were all single mothers and were living every day with the stress I had just discovered. For them, there was no end in sight.

My project work there should have lasted a couple of weeks, but somehow the women in the office kept destroying the work I did, thus extending my contract. To this day I don't know if they were helping me or just utterly incompetent, but it was nice to have some income.

## Actually, Dad, I Was Really Asking for Money

*Desperate and having no other plan, I commiserated with my father. I had resigned myself to working two jobs and hoping for things to get better. And for the moment, like the dedicated, single moms I worked with, I would have to stay at a job I detested but that paid relatively well for a part-time gig.*

*"That's what a lot of people have to do every day, son," my father sympathized. He had lost his job due to illness and a recession years ago, and I could hear echoes of that memory in his tone. But then he stopped, and as he had done so many times before he caught me off guard. "So this is who you are then?"*

*I had no idea what he meant.*

*"Who you are during stress," he explained, "that's you. That's the real you. Is this who you are? Because if it is, okay, especially if you can accept that. But just know that when things get better, and you feel more secure, how you acted during these tough times will define who you are. It will be how you see yourself—how your wife and how your children ultimately see you."*

*That night, I couldn't get to sleep. It wasn't the money worries or not having a stable job, it was deciding if this was who I was. In the morning, I decided it wasn't. I quit the part-time job and let the president know he was a jerk for abusing the women who worked for him. I tried to confront him, without letting the women in the office hear me and make them feel bad. Once I got over the fact that I was locked inside a bulletproof room and that no one could hear me scream, I said my piece.*

*I walked out and I focused on finding the right job. I took every freelance gig I could, and got lucky. My sister-in-law was having computer problems at her job, and her boss told her to find someone who could help. The owner of the company was incredibly nice, I could work at night, and there was plenty to do, so at least food and rent would be taken care of for now.*

*I spent my days looking for the right work. My sister told me about a position at a nearby company—and I had noticed the ad in the newspaper (yes, this was a long time ago)—but couldn't find it. I decided to track it down. I eventually found it while going over old newspapers at the library. While waiting for a response I sent out a hundred resumes and interviewed at ten different positions. Finally, the hiring person from that lost ad called, and I got an interview. I had a 104-degree fever for my second interview, but sucked it up and nailed it (turns out that if you don't drink water, you can't look sweaty). By the first of December I was employed, had insurance, and was doing something I wanted to do. Yes, I was fortunate. Yes, it was a relatively short period of time. But what mattered was that I defined who I was during that time, and it made all the difference for the rest of my life.*

## Desperate Times Call for Genuine People

How does this apply to business? When we sign on a new client at my company, we tell them they have rights: "In any relationship, things will go wrong. The measure of a company—or a person—is how they will react when things go wrong. This outlines how we will react." I want my clients to know what I will do if something bad happens and they feel vulnerable. Will I have their back and do the right thing? We promise upfront we will.

For employees, I have more faith in the ones who have made a potential job-losing mistake, and survived it, than those who have been perfect. Sure, I would love perfect people, but knowing what someone will do when they realize they've made a mistake that should get them fired tells me everything I need to know.

It is too easy to lose sight of who you are when things go badly. Even nations have abandoned their values when they felt threatened or close to total defeat; people can make bad decisions if they feel they are desperate and have no way out. But thanks to my father, when things have gone bad, I have been able to stop a moment and ask, "Is this who I really am?"

So who are you? And who do you want to be?

BEFORE YOU GO TOO FAR DOWN
THE WRONG ROAD, THINK ABOUT THE
FACT THAT YOUR CHILDREN ARE
WATCHING. WHAT LESSONS WOULD
THEY LEARN IF THEY COULD SEE WHAT
YOU WERE DOING RIGHT NOW?

LESSON THREE:

# NEVER FORGET YOUR CHILDREN ARE WATCHING, OR YOUR NAME IS MY NAME.

Josie was a bundle of raw energy and focus. Smart and attractive, well-educated and resourceful, she came from a poor family and worked her way through a prestigious college. She followed her boyfriend out to the West Coast when he got a great job at a Yellow Pages company (right now any reader under twenty-five is asking "What the hell is a Yellow Pages company?"), and was soon working as my marketing director. She had an uncanny ability to develop ways to get new clients and make money. In fact, whenever I tried to quote a price to a customer she would admonish me, knowing that we could get more. Eventually, I let her do the talking and our margins shot up.

Then one day a client mentioned that one of their divisions was having an issue. They published a magazine of 900 numbers (cue the millennial: "What is a 900 number?"). Basically, the magazine showed pictures of women in bikinis or lingerie holding a phone. Guys (or mostly guys—okay, only lonely guys) would call in, feel like they made a connection with a woman, and talk for hours. Then the phone bill came and they realized they were paying five dollars a minute to be told how special they were. Nothing illegal, but it wasn't exactly a great business model, either.

"The problem is," our client explained, "the company that creates the layouts and gets the magazine ready for print every month, screwed it up. The flats have to be at the printers on Monday, and we have nothing."

"Monday? Are you kidding?" I laughed. "It's Thursday."

"I know. I am hoping this miracle digital stuff you guys sell can do it. Can you?"

Josie looked at me intently and I nodded. "We can do it," she said, "but it won't be cheap. You need to know that now."

"How not cheap?" our client asked.

Josie looked at me, making sure I didn't answer. "Let us review what you have and then we can give you an answer." Our client nodded and we were on our way. By Sunday night we had the thirty-two-page magazine and negatives ready for delivery. I had worked three days straight through. I wanted to charge a hundred dollars an hour for my time (a huge amount back then), but Josie laughed. "We need to add in my overhead."

We presented the negatives and the bill to our client, an unmerciful (in my mind) $10,000. We were into the deal a few hundred dollars for negatives and $4,000 in my time at my hundred-dollar an hour rate.

The client not only didn't blink, he was grateful. "Anyone in your position would have doubled that, knowing I had no choice. Thank you for playing fairly. That's what we paid our other company on a regular basis. Do you guys want the project?"

"How often do you do this, and what is the standard turnaround time?" Josie asked, trying to suck in the drool that was forming around her mouth without making a huge noise.

"It's a monthly magazine. Our former vendor needed two weeks for turnaround. We can live with that. I can get you the contract today."

We had just stumbled onto a high-profit, $120,000-a-year account. With our technology, we could do this, make them happy, and collect a huge profit. There was only one problem: I could hear my niece, my sweet little four-year-old, adorable niece, asking me "What do you do for a living, Uncle Ron?" "Oh, I help suck the money out of gullible guys' wallets."

Josie looked at me, sickened that I was not jumping for joy.

"We need time to think about it," I said. "We'll give you an answer on Monday."

On the drive back to the office, I was glad that Josie was from a state where people didn't typically own guns.

"You have ten minutes, you commie bastard, to tell me why you don't want to take this sweetheart account," Josie said through clenched teeth.

I need twenty," I said, "it involves a Len story."

## The New Cleaning Guy is Great, But a Little Touchy

*"I got fired today," my father said matter-of-factly. My father got fired (or quit) a lot, so losing a job was not exactly the bombshell that it was on TV. Since he always started a new job days later, it was never really a dramatic event in my mind. Growing up, I assumed everyone changed jobs every few months. He was an educated engineer and worked in the computer field. With more openings than qualified people, unemployment was not a concern. To my father, longevity, seniority, and retirement were not concerns either.*

*"It seems," he started to explain, although no one asked, "that my supervisor decided our area was not clean enough. The cleaning people come in once a week, but the floor was often littered with computer parts and debris. Seems that was a problem for him."*

*"I can see that," my mother interjected. It was always interesting to me to see how unaffected my mother was when my father quit a job. She had worked ten years at the same factory, and you'd*

think she'd go crazy when my father changed jobs. But she didn't. I was fortunate enough to marry a woman a lot like that, who never blinked when I said stupid things like "Hey, I want to leave my good paying corporate officer's job and start a new company doing something I know nothing about."

"Yeah, me, too." My father continued. "Problem was, Henry decided that I should be the one to keep things clean. So he asked me—told me—I needed to clean the place."

"Why you?" my sister asked.

"Good question. I asked him that. He said it was his decision and he just picked me."

"That's not fair," she added.

"No, it's not." My father looked over at my brother, the only person at the table more interested in the bistec empanizado we were eating than his story. The look of disgust on my father's face faded quickly as he continued.

"So, I told him, if we all took turns, I could see that. But if it was just me, this was not going to end the way he thought it would. But he said 'Do it, and don't threaten me.' So I did it."

We all stopped for a moment and looked at my dad. For all of his faults, for all of his ill-tempered rants, long stories, crazy flights of fancy on weekends when we all just wanted to sleep in, the one thing my father was not was a coward. And to everyone sitting at that table, it was cowardly to do something that was unfair and capricious just because someone in authority said so. As kids, we didn't understand that parents needed to make rent, feed their children, and pay healthcare. But we knew parents set examples, and my father's example was always that the best way to make a bully back off was to make him (or her) regret they ever lived.

"What?" we collectively gasped.

"I did it. In fact, I cleaned that office better than anyone had ever cleaned the office before. I picked up. I swept the floor. I cleaned the refrigerator and threw out the moldy food. I even went to the bathroom and emptied the trash bins. After two hours I had four giant bags of trash and the cleanest work area in the company."

We were lost. Not to mention, we weren't quite sure why he would get fired for being such a great cleaning person.

"And then, I walked into Henry's office. I left the door open and asked my fellow employees to come in. I explained what Henry had asked and how I took it to heart. I even admonished them for letting the place get so dirty. 'I even found rat crap on the floor,' I said. 'We can't live with all of this filth.' Then I emptied all of the trash bags on Henry's desk. Maybe a little on Henry. Poor guy, it was disgusting.

"And that's how I got fired. But we all got a good laugh. Well, except for Henry. He looked like a jerk and a fool. He got a little angry and wanted to shout at me, but I reminded him how since I was fired, shouting would be personal, not business. 'Did he really want to make it personal?' I asked; he didn't."

We all laughed.

*My father also got a nice severance, because when HR heard the whole story, they weren't really happy with Henry. They might have been concerned about being sued. They even offered my father his job back, but my dad was happy to take the money and leave with his dignity intact.*

*The next day, as my mother made me lunch and we were alone, I brought up the story and laughed. My mother admonished me. "Your father really liked that job. He liked the company. He wasn't happy to leave," she explained.*

*"He could have kept the job," I said.*

*"I think he wanted more to teach Henry a lesson," she said. "He has a bad temper, and he probably could have yelled at Henry and Henry would have backed down. But then he would have just found someone else to pick on. I think your father was more concerned with how you guys would see him, if he didn't stick up for others."*

*"I don't understand what this has to do with what happened," I asked.*

*"If your father would have kept the job and just had someone else do the cleaning, that would have not been right. Henry needed to learn a lesson. And he wanted to make sure you guys learned the lesson. So that is why he acted the way he did and then told you what happened."*

*"Because of us? I thought he just relished showing the jerk up."*

*"Well, that too," she laughed. "But it is important to your father that you guys are watching him as an example. Someday*

*you are going to have your own family and they will inherit your name. If he screws up the name, or if he does things that make you think less of him, it goes on to the next generation. His name is your name, and your name will be your children's name. That's why it was important for him to do the right thing. And the right thing was to stop an idiot from being abusive, not to just defend himself."*

*I am not sure I understood the lesson then, but later in life—when I was confronted with forks in the road where I could take the easy road or the right road—I often thought about the fact that his name is my name. When my children were born, I kept thinking about that, and about the fact that my children were watching me. I want to say that I always did the right thing, but that would be a lie (and after the chapter on lying, you would know I was lying). But it did make me think about my actions, and I hope I got it right more times than I got it wrong.*

*Even to this day, with my children grown and having their own children, I know my children are watching me to learn how to act, as parents or employees or just people. And that is why I was not comfortable telling my niece that I helped take advantage of lonely people.*

## You Are So Not Getting Any Tonight

Josie was disgusted. "I like your father," she said. "But what he said does not apply here. We are not doing anything wrong. We are not selling porn or doing anything illegal. We are providing layouts. It is not our job to judge what they do with it."

"I'm not judging," I explained. "They can do what they want. I just don't want to help them. I don't want my daughter posing in a magazine like that, and I don't want my son calling in and thinking that is a normal relationship. I can't do it. Would you want to be in that magazine?"

Josie shook her head. "I don't have the body for it. But if those models want to be in it, I don't care. We are talking a lot of money. You used to edit a newspaper. You don't drink, right?"

I nodded. Again, I wasn't morally against it, I just hated the taste of alcohol and didn't like being drunk.

"Well, you accepted beer ads, so what's the difference?"

"Actually, I didn't," I corrected her. "As editor I didn't run ads for beer companies, or a few other industries I didn't agree with."

Josie looked at me like I had just confessed to the Manson murders. "You communist. You don't get to decide who advertises in a newspaper, or what clients do with what you provide. That goes against everything capitalism stands for. Or the Constitution. What is wrong with you?" (As you might have figured out by now, I get asked this a lot.)

"My company," I offered meekly. "It's not about stopping them from doing it. I just don't want to help. I don't want to set that example for my niece. Or some day for my kids."

Josie was furious. "So we are not taking the account because you don't want your niece to think you're a bad guy."

"Yes."

"I just don't get it. I don't see anything wrong with doing this."

"And that's the point," I said, regaining my logic. "You don't think this is wrong, and that is okay. But I do. If this was your company and you did it, I would understand. But it's me, it's my company, and I do have a problem with it. That's why I can't do it. It's about doing things we are proud of."

Josie was too angry to care about the distinction. "Any chance of changing your mind?"

"No."

"Well, at least I know you will never have to worry about having children with me," she mumbled as she lit up a cigarette and stared out the window.

## Things Are Easier to Explain
## When You Feel in the Right

We are tempted often during the course of a day. Sometimes with money, sometimes with not being bothered, or just taking the easy way. But before you go too far down the wrong road, think about the fact that your children are watching. What lessons would they learn if they could see what you were doing right now?

If you don't have children, you are *not* off the hook. You likely still have someone that loves you or looks up to you.

In my opinion, having a conscience is what keeps us from taking the road most traveled and getting into real trouble. For some people it may be an animated talking cricket, and for others it's an angel on their shoulder; for me it was my father and his admonishment about our responsibility to our family and to others. So respectfully, and with all the faults of a very, very defective human, I offer these things to apply in your life:

1. *Consider what you are about to do.* Does it sully your name? Would you want your children to know you did it? Your spouse? If you are too embarrassed to tell anyone about what you are about to do, you probably shouldn't do it.

2. *Sometimes it's others who give us the strength to do what we should.* I have a bad heart. When I eat vegan and don't ingest oils, I feel great—alive and healthy. When I eat crap, I feel like crap. When I lack the intestinal fortitude to pass up a cheeseburger or rib eye steak, my wife gives me the look that says, "Do you really want to do that?" It is how people we love help make us better. Unfortunately, a lot of decisions happen when no one is looking. Reminding yourself that someone is watching (even when they aren't) can give you the strength to do the right thing.

3. *In work, and in life, it is easy to just get along.* Don't make waves. Keep your head down. But ultimately, getting along isn't the end all, be all. I doubt that many people who make it to their deathbed think, "Hey, I went along with everything, so no regrets." Maybe you have to make waves and stand up just to teach your own kids a lesson.

This was a hard chapter to write. I am not trying to say that you should do what I think is right, but what *you* think is right. I can't say I always lived up to my own standard, but at least I know a standard exists and there is a reason I need to uphold it. My father did for me, so I could be proud of him.

Hopefully, my kids will be proud of me (especially when I wear loud shirts and sing Billy Joel songs from my convertible at the top of my very unmusical voice).

FEAR MAKES US SEE ENEMIES EVERYWHERE, DOUBT OUR FRIENDS, AND LOOK FOR WAYS TO DIVIDE US FROM OTHER PEOPLE. FEAR MAKES US FEEL LESS THAN WHAT WE ARE.

# BONUS LESSON:

# *HAGATE HOMBRE* (OR *MUJER*).

It was still early in the morning, but you could already feel the heat seeping out of the sand. Beautiful, rugged, and intolerant, Joshua Tree National Park was located just miles from where Marines trained for desert combat. If you know anything about Marines, you know they never train anywhere pleasant.

For our family it was a weekend day trip. We drove to the Mojave Desert to do some hiking and see some wildlife. By "hiking" I mean walk miles in triple-digit heat, and by "see some wildlife" I mean buzzards flying overhead while we begged my father for water.

The desert was one of my father's favorite places, whether it was desolate and unspoiled like Joshua Tree, or glitzy and irritatingly kitschy as Las Vegas was, is, and always will be. Oddly, as I grew older I, too, liked the desert, albeit more from the view of my two-seater convertible than stumbling down a rocky path.

"Okay, everyone have water?" my father asked, not really waiting for or expecting a response. We nodded and checked the laughably small canisters of life-saving liquid we were given. While my father droned down his list of items to remember, I quietly imagined how much liquid was inside my brother. *No one would miss him*, I thought.

My attention was then ripped away by my father's next survival topic.

"You might find rattlesnakes, cougars, scorpions, things like that on the trek. The important thing to remember if you run into something dangerous is not to panic."

I immediately started panicking. What the hell kind of place was this? They never had that speech on the Matterhorn at Disneyland. As my father continued listing 1,001 ways to die in the desert, I think he could sense the anxiety welling up in all of us. My sister could feel her skin crawling with imaginary tarantulas.

"Stay calm. Think before you move," he explained. "Sometimes you need to stay still. Sometimes you need to walk away slowly, but screaming and running never helps. You can't outrun a cougar and a coiled snake can lunge faster than you can retreat. Understand? Think. Don't panic."

A mutiny was not far away.

As he spoke, he slowly moved back and a small branch brushed against his pant leg. Whatever he imagined that branch was, it caused him to scream, jump up, and run. "You're on your own!" was all we heard as he disappeared from view. At first we were startled, looking for an invisible rattler, and then the humor kicked in. By the time my father returned, we were exhausted from convulsive laughter. It took a good thirty minutes before we were composed enough to begin, finish—and enjoy—our trek through Hades National Park.

At the time, I assumed my father had been bitch-slapped by karma, showing him to be less logical and fearless than he claimed to be. But as I grew older, I realized the theatrics were there to defuse a tense situation and to acknowledge that while we were all scared and uncomfortable, fear is something you can learn to manage. He repeated this lesson over and over. In fact, it echoed one of his favorite sayings: "*Hagate hombre*" or "be a man" (or woman); he didn't discriminate in his expectations of his children.

While it has sexist overtones (and given his age and culture, the saying was probably more than a little tainted with machismo), to me it came to mean something different. Face your fear. Think. Act the way you want to act and to be seen, not the way your fear compels you to act. Throughout my life, when fear was holding me back—fear of dying, fear of getting hurt, or fear of just losing—I could hear my father's voice saying "*Hagate hombre.*" Many times it wasn't metaphorical—he actually was yelling "*¡Hagate hombre!*" at me.

It's easy to pretend you are not afraid. We have all seen the bullies, the false bravado of people who try to avoid being hurt or show real emotion. But there is a difference between pretending to not be afraid and confronting your fear.

I don't like social situations. I can present on stage or teach a class, but the thought of being at a party trying to make small talk is terrifying. I invariably say stupid things or trip and fall. My father's remedy for this affliction? *Hagate hombre.* Well, that and some added advice: acknowledge to yourself that you are uncomfortable. Realize that you are likely to say or do something stupid. Act calm on the outside and take a moment to think before you talk or move. That advice helps with my social anxiety. I still don't like it, but I can at least get through a cocktail party without spilling a soda on my wife's beautiful dress or yelling out to my client's wife, Tourette's-style, "Wow, you have gained a lot of weight!"

*Hagate hombre* (or *mujer*) means even more to me now than I am older. Fear is the mind-killer. It stops us from doing what we want or enjoying what we have. It keeps us from acting the way we should. Sure, evolution has built fear into us to keep us alive, but the response that kept us from being eaten by a pack of wolves can be over-exaggerated in a situation where the worst that can happen is that your Tesla gets repossessed. "Be a man" was my father's not-so-gentle reminder to think first and be scared later. And sometimes just taking a moment to think allows you to act beyond your fear.

If you lose who you are over fear, you stop living. You stop having a moral compass. It's harder to do the right thing when you are scared. It's not because you don't know the right thing, but because you can't overcome that fear that numbs your brain and makes you believe that losing an argument or getting on a plane is exactly like being eaten by a tiger. And fear is very personal; there are people who will rush onto a battlefield or life-threatening situation but are hesitant to confront a boss.

Confronting your fear also means not using fear to motivate others. Fear is a negative emotion but, unfortunately, one that can be used effectively to get people to react. I just don't think it works for very long. Or gets the desired effects. It also inspires less-reputable people to drive us in a direction we shouldn't go. While we all sometimes use fear in small ways to get what we want ("Go to bed or Santa won't come;" "Clean up your room or you'll be grounded;" "Do what I say or you're fired"), in reality, people who care about us use love and encouragement much more than they use fear to motivate. If fear is how your supervisor, spouse, coworker, president, or governor motivates you, you can be certain whatever they are telling you is not likely in your best interest.

Fear makes us see enemies everywhere, doubt our friends, and look for ways to divide us from other people. Fear makes us feel less than what we are. People who lead and command with fear want you to be small so that you will come running to them. After all, if you weren't scared, alone, and feeling vulnerable, why would you ever listen to someone whose only ability is to make someone else a boogeyman, or prey on our darkest motives?

"*Hagate mujer*" and stop to think when you are afraid: Is this really that scary? Do I really need to overreact, or should I just take a moment and breathe and think this out?

My father once asked me what I would do if a large biker came at me with a crowbar. (Again, these are the types of conversations I had growing up.)

"Hit first, hit hard, aim for the eyes, and then run like hell," I replied. I think we had actually rehearsed this once or twice.

"Exactly," he said. "Now what would you do if a small child came at you with a toy gun?"

"Nothing."

"Would you hurt him?" he asked.

"Of course not," I laughed.

"Exactly. Not every threat," he explained, "is life-threatening. But when you act out of fear, even a small child can seem threatening."

It's easy to say don't be afraid, but that's not feasible or even the lesson here. Be afraid, but don't act afraid. Don't be craven and cowardly. Stop. Think. Breathe. Put your fear into perspective for a moment and then be a man. Or a woman. And for God's sake, if the man behind the curtain is yelling at you to be afraid, just change the channel.

# A FINAL THOUGHT

So now that you have read this book, what is the point? If you are asking at this stage, my guess is you are doing so while standing in the return line at Barnes & Noble. But if you are asking metaphorically, the answer is: My father took the time to teach me lessons in life that no one else seemed intent on showing me. Not everyone has a father, mother, or a mentor; some people don't have *good* parents or *good* role models. Luckily, and through no deserving actions of my own, I did. The things my father taught me made my life better, and they helped me succeed in many of the things I have tried in life.

More importantly, I have come across many people who don't get what they want in life or business and don't know why. After years of watching people, I believe the answer is often *because no one ever told them how to succeed.*

Finally, this book is a very personal way to say thank you to my father. Success means a lot of things to different people, whether it is financial independence, influence, fame, or just ending your life better than you started it. For me, a big part of what

I call fulfillment is having had a sense of control over my life. In almost any situation I had the skills to handle what came my way. I owe that to my father.

I hope in a small way, this book will help you feel the same.

On another note: I'd love to hear your feedback on how this book has helped you, for good or bad. Visit ronzayas.com/lenmaster and give me your feedback. For those who do—and who want to—I'll put you on my beta group to read my next book before it comes out.

# ACKNOWLEDGMENTS

It is almost trite to say that nothing important ever gets done without the help of others, but sometimes you need to state the obvious anyway. I acknowledge and thank the friends, family, business partners, and publishers who helped bring this book to reality:

Janise Marie, for believing in the book early on and working hard to find the right publisher.

David Hofstede, for the patient editing, proofing, feedback, and early encouragement.

Maddie S., Anthony Z., and the rest of the team at Post Hill. You made this process easier than I have ever experienced, and I am grateful for the improvements you have made to the book.

Bridget DiRico, for always reading every manuscript I sent your way whether you wanted to or not.

# ABOUT THE AUTHOR

Photo courtesy of T Taylor Photography

An experienced CEO, Ron co-founded 360 BC Group in 2004 and quickly grew it into a successful online marketing agency that caters to Fortune 500, major municipalities, and small business clients. Prior to 360, he spent ten years as chief marketing officer for the world's largest franchisor of printing and small business services. He is a frequent mentor or board member to innovative start-ups.

Ron has also been a founder or key partner in multiple successful start-ups, including a business that focuses on social media child protection, and founded one of the nation's first digital graphics companies.

Ron is a frequent speaker and blogger on the future of online technology, marketing, or how to protect the privacy of children and individuals on the Internet. He has delivered presentations on these vital topics to the Federal Trade Commission and the National Association of Attorneys General. He is a licensed pilot and has published numerous books on marketing and small business management.